SIMPLE FENG SHUI

ANCIENT PRINCIPLES
TO BRING LOVE, JOY,
AND PROSPERITY
INTO YOUR LIFE

SHAWNE MITCHELL
WITH STEPHANIE GUNNING

GRAMERCY BOOKS
NEW YORK

This 2004 edition is published by Gramercy Books, an imprint of Random House Value Publishing, a division of Random House, Inc., New York, by arrangement with Career Press.

Gramercy is a registered trademark and the colophon is a trademark of Random House, Inc.

Random House
New York • Toronto • London • Sydney • Auckland
www.randomhouse.com

Typeset by Stacey A. Farkas

Printed and bound in the United States

Library of Congress Cataloging-in-Publication Data

Mitchell, Shawne, 1958-
[Exploring feng shui]
    Simple feng shui : ancient principles to bring love, joy, and prosperity into your life/ Shawne Mitchell with Stephanie Gunning.
        p. cm.
    Originally published: Exploring feng shui. Franklin Lakes, NJ : New Page Books, c2002.
    Includes bibliographical references and index.
    ISBN 0-517-22296-5
    1. Feng shui. I. Gunning, Stephanie, 1962- II. Title.

BF1779.F4M58 2004
133.3'337—dc22

                                                        2003049394

10 9 8 7 6 5 4 3 2 1

For
Travis and Austin

Acknowledgments

I would like to acknowledge and express my love and gratitude to Stephanie Gunning, an extraordinary writer and angel being, for her exemplary writing, collaboration, friendship, and support. You are my "patron saint!"

I am grateful for the love and lives of my sons, Travis and Austin Cook. Thank you for sharing your vision, insight, humor, and patience with Mom!

I want to thank Stefany Evans, my agent, for her unshakable faith in this work and sharing her friendship, guidance, enthusiasm, and commitment. You are wonderful!

My thanks to Y.S. Kim for his wonderful illustrations.

Also, much thanks to editor Mike Lewis at New Page Books.

My gratitude and thanks to my friend, Arielle Ford, for her generous and authentic support in sharing wisdom, transformation, and love.

I am immensely grateful for the support, insight, and kindness of Denise Linn, whose work and beingness exemplify sacred grace.

I also want to thank my parents in heaven, Nona and King, and my brothers, Richard, Chris, Mitch, Ryan, and Dan, and their families for their constant love and support. I am, indeed, blessed.

Finally, I must thank my Divine Within for compelling me to go ever deeper in my spiritual quest to share a lifestyle aligned with the soul.

Contents

Introduction: What Is Feng Shui?   9

1. Schools of Feng Shui   19

2. Balance and Harmony   29

3. The 5 Elemental Forces of Creation   41

4. Mapping Your Environment   57

5. Remedies for Common Problems   75

6. Evaluating Your Surroundings   105

7. Evaluating Your Home and Garden   121

8. Evaluating Your Business   143

9. When You Need an Expert   163

Recommended Reading   179

Index   183

About the Author   191

Introduction

What Is Feng Shui?

Jackie was an entrepreneur. She had a good product and a committed staff, and she spent long hours and lots of money wooing and networking with prospective clients. So she couldn't figure out why she wasn't happier and her company more successful despite many years of effort. By the time she came to me for a feng shui consultation, she felt discouraged and was close to shutting her business down. After visiting her office, I suggested she move her desk to a different corner of the room, the "wealth" zone on the feng shui map called the bagua. I also had her turn it around so that she could see and welcome people coming through the door. Besides repositioning her furniture, we strategically placed several objects around her office representing prosperity and beneficial people. Five days later, out of the blue, Jackie received an offer from a former business associate to purchase her company for a handsome profit.

Another of my clients felt terribly lonely after the loss of her husband. When Barbara asked me to come to her home, hanging in her bedroom I found a large portrait of a solitary woman sitting in lonely repose within a lush garden setting. Although it was beautiful, the image was also symbolic of her current emotional state. It seemed to me that she was subconsciously maintaining her isolation by surrounding herself in her intimate space with objects that reinforced her grief and loneliness. So I suggested that she replace the painting with a romantic piece of artwork featuring a loving couple. Three months after making this simple change, Barbara phoned to let me know that she had met a wonderful man and fallen in love.

In my practice as a feng shui consultant, I have seen exciting transformations and opportunities such as Jackie's and Barbara's occur on a regular basis. That is the essential magic of feng shui. When we set a clear intention based on our heart's true desire and align our environments to support it, fantastic shifts can and do happen. It is intangible and seemingly illogical, yet over the past 20 years I have learned to accept these events as reliable and even inevitable.

Although feng shui (pronounced *fung shway*) may seem mysterious at first, once you begin learning and working with its principles, I know you will experience its benefits firsthand. As your confidence builds, I am certain that feng shui will become a valuable ally in taking control of your life and steering your destiny.

Is your life creating you, or are you creating your life?

Do you sometimes feel out of control, as though the whims of life and livelihood have caught you by the tail? Have your dreams and aspirations been crushed by the demands of your day-to-day reality? Perhaps that is why you have been drawn to this book and the study of feng shui. You want to change your life and find ways to bring into it everything you are dreaming about: love, joy, peace, and abundance.

Would you roll your eyes or laugh if I told you that you were already living the life you chose?

There is an old adage: Where attention goes, energy flows. What you think about most is generally what gets created in your reality.

Intangibles—your thoughts and ideas—are given form in the world through your actions, both directly and indirectly, consciously and subconsciously.

Please take this opportunity to look around and consider where you have been putting your attention. Maybe you bought a house because it was spacious and had a lot of bedrooms or took a job because it paid well. There are always reasons. But now, in addition to all the benefits of space and income, you also have higher taxes and greater expenses, and you must work overtime. These indirect results are linked to your original actions and reasons for taking them. They are part of the life you created. Whether you are aware of it or not, your world is a reflection of what is going on inside you.

Every moment holds an opportunity to choose. You can choose what you place your attention on and you can choose how you respond to what you experience. Choosing is the process of setting an intention. Your intention in one moment shapes your actions in the next moment, and what you intend in that next moment shapes the moment that follows it. Intention leads the flow of your life. Therefore, to create change you must change your thoughts. Making conscious choices puts you in charge of creating your life.

Feng shui is the art of conscious creation. It is the act of working with physical objects in the environment in such a way that they support what you want. By paying attention and making your world an intentional mirror, you can create new outcomes. As within, so without. The reverse is also true.

The invisible force of life: chi

The guiding philosophy of feng shui is that everything in the universe, including every one of us, is made of the same basic energy. This universal energy known as chi (pronounced *chee*) is alive and it has intelligence. Because on this most fundamental level everything is in relationship with everything else, whenever anything changes, everything else also changes as a result. Chi constantly ebbs and flows around and through us in ever-shifting patterns and levels of intensity.

Modern science authenticated what the ancient Chinese art of feng shui has recognized for more than 4,000 years through the discovery that all matter and non-matter are composed of subatomic particles of energy. Quantum physicists have since done experiments that show that these infinitesimally small bits of energy literally respond to thought, changing their behavior depending on where and how researchers focus their attention. This revelation affirms the awesome power of feng shui.

Imagine that a bubble of energy surrounds your body and extends 10 feet in every direction. As you move through the world, people and objects unavoidably pass through this bubble. Where your energy bubble intersects with the bubbles of others, a sort of co-mingling process takes place in which your energy responds to theirs and their energy responds to yours. Intangible thoughts and feelings can be communicated through these fields from person to person and by entering different spaces.

If the man sitting next to you on the bus were angry, his energy would feel "angry." You could read his state of being through your energy field even though you never held a conversation. If you walked into a church or temple where people have been praying for centuries, you likewise might pick up the energy signature of "peace" and "devotion" embedded in its walls and altars. The presence of anger and devotion would ripple into and through your field. You might also become angry or peaceful just by being exposed and responding to the energy of these emotions and thoughts.

And perhaps your energy bubble extends farther than 10 feet. Perhaps it is unlimited in scope, because at the subatomic level your personal energy is merely a drop in an entire sea of universal chi. In that case, every aspect of the world at large would impact you to a measurable degree. Everyone and everything on the planet in this scenario can be seen as interrelated and interdependent.

I invite you to keep an open mind and consider the potential that this vision holds: We are all connected, part of the oneness of the universe. It is a point of orientation on which mystics and scientists, faith and logic can agree. Although feng shui is not actually considered a spiritual practice or religion, it is a subtle and intuitive art that may ultimately enhance your spiritual beliefs. Furthermore, it is clear that the principles of energy are operating in our lives whether or not we are consciously attuned to them. Through feng shui, we can purposefully regulate the flow of positive energy in our environment and as a result enhance our lives.

What you will learn in this book

The practice of feng shui is based on the premise that the quality of the chi that moves around and through our homes, offices, and neighborhoods affects our well-being. The quality of chi can be expressed through form, color, texture, or the feeling it generates. Chi permeates everything, whether the source is natural or man-made, animate or inanimate. Feng shui teaches us to harness this vital life force, which is the most important influence on our lives for better or for worse.

Our personal chi is in a constant interplay with environmental chi. Chi that flows well through any environment is beneficial. It contributes to health, joy, love, and prosperity. Chi that is obstructed or stagnant produces harmful consequences. It contributes to disease, negativity, conflict, and scarcity. Too much chi can be as much of a problem as too little chi. Crosscurrents can also generate patterns of conflict.

Feng shui can be likened to a language that has its own special grammar and vocabulary. Once you grasp these rules and building blocks, you can begin to read and refashion the invisible energy where you live and work to manifest success and abundance, find and maintain loving and nurturing relationships, and enjoy true happiness and health.

In this book you will first learn the fundamentals of the art of feng shui. Feng shui uses the primary balance of opposites, the yin and yang energy of a space—dark and light, feminine and masculine, receptive and active, soft and hard, round and angular—to establish harmony. It also recognizes five elements that hold and move energy in different ways: fire, earth, metal, water, and wood. What the senses can perceive—color, texture, aroma, simplicity, and symbolism—are some of the most dynamic components of the balance of yin and yang and the elements.

Starting with a basic mapping device called the bagua, you will learn which of the areas in your environment are connected to Journey and Career, Self-Wisdom and Knowledge, Family and Health, Prosperity and Abundance, Fame and Reputation, Marriage and Relationships, Children and Creativity, and Helpful People and Travel. You also will be given the tools to change problem zones into life-affirming zones of opportunity, by moving your furniture, making repairs, eliminating clutter, installing mirrors, adding more and better lighting, growing plants, and performing rituals for clearing stale and stagnant energy, among other straightforward strategies. Individual chapters will be devoted to evaluating and improving the feng shui of your home and garden, your office, and your surrounding neighborhood. A final chapter will address special circumstances that require professional assistance.

Before you can begin to improve or remedy the energy flow in your environment, you need to have a basic understanding of how the Chinese view the universe.

The fundamentals of feng shui

Balance

The first fundamental principle of feng shui philosophy is the concept of balance. The world is filled with pairs of opposites that fall into two categories known as *yin* and *yang*. Yin qualities are feminine, receptive, dark, cool, moist, and round. Yang qualities are masculine, assertive, light, hot, dry, and angular. When yin and yang are in balance, the result is harmony.

Lisa was working on a doctorate in psychology and struggling to write her thesis. She had set aside a wonderful room for the purpose of writing. It had big windows with a view of the Pacific Ocean that provided lots of light, high ceilings, and a fireplace. Nonetheless, she did not feel inspired. It seemed difficult for her to access her inner resources—the realm of her imagination—in that space. Whatever was being created there was either going out the window or up the chimney.

Lisa got in touch with me. During our consultation we worked to incorporate more yin qualities to balance the abundance of yang in her writing room. She repainted the walls with a watery blue-green color to cool them and reupholstered her furniture with organic fabrics designed with floral motifs. She placed large flowering plants by the windows and set a large ornamental fan in front of the fireplace.

In the end she found the space much more nurturing and fertile and felt that it had a smoother flow of energy, thus encouraging the flow of her ideas as she wrote.

5 elemental forces of creation

The second fundamental principle of feng shui pertains to the natural cycles of creation and destruction. Everything in the universe may be classified as wood, fire, earth, metal, or water. These five elemental forces denote the various ways that chi interacts and becomes transformed. For instance, wood represents upward growth and progress. Fire represents heat and expansion. Earth denotes stability and dependability. Metal represents strength. Water is symbolic of fluidity and movement. Sometimes these elements interact in productive patterns and other times in destructive patterns. They also correspond to seasonal cycles and the directions of the compass.

Mark, another client of mine, wanted to improve his standing in the company where he worked. During our consultation, I suggested that a specific corner of his office would be a good place for a water element, such as an aquarium. Water would help activate the chi, thus reinforcing his career intention. We discussed various possible features that could do the trick. He decided on a small fountain, because it would be easier for him to tend than a fish tank. Within a month, he received a promotion.

Mapping the environment

The third fundamental principle of feng shui is the idea of mapping the environment. What do the color of our front doors, the location of our bedrooms, and the trees and shrubs in our front yards have to do with our personal well-being? Our homes are mirrors of our selves. They reflect our interests, our beliefs, our values, our spirits, and our passions. They are the intersection between the inner world and the outer world.

Our homes are also suffused with our personal energy. They are not just a composite of materials thrown together for shelter and comfort. Every centimeter, whether an empty space or one filled with solid objects, contains an infinite number of energy fields. These fields are physical, emotional, mental, and etheric. And they are constantly moving, swirling, mixing, and interacting.

According to feng shui, different areas of the home correspond literally to different parts of your life. They can be mapped using a template called the bagua. There is a zone for work, a zone for relationships, and a zone for health, among others. When you change and activate the energy in a zone, you can change the part of your life that it represents. You are no less your home in an energetic sense than you are your body.

How to approach this book

Nowadays we live longer and experience perhaps more than a hundred times more events than our ancestors did only a century ago. Everyday life is complicated. It ebbs and flows. There are times of expansion and times of contraction. Most of us can expect to face occasional stresses and challenges. Feng shui should not be considered a panacea to the difficulties of life. Although it is a valuable ally, it is not going to solve all your problems. It isn't a magic pill. Nonetheless, it can assist and support you during times of stress. It does help you focus and amplify your intentions.

Intention

Recognizing and understanding the universal life force, chi, is perhaps the most fundamental principle of feng shui. No less important, however, is the concept of setting clear intentions. Even if you understand energy and how it flows, you must have a goal in mind in order to harness that energy for manifestation. The principle of intention transforms passion and thought into action. Therefore the clearer and more committed you are about your intention, the stronger the energy that gets focused on your desire. As you will learn, the tools of feng shui work best when you are purposeful. They become anchoring devices that attract, enhance, and stabilize energy.

The spirit of play

Approach this book as an innocent child. Children's play helps them synthesize, manage, and create their worlds. With feng shui you can adopt the same spirit of play, exploring the energy of your life. Use what you find here to experiment and try out ideas, imagining and testing new ways of life to see whether or not they suit you.

You do not have to believe in feng shui for it to work. Consider it a symbolic gesture, a way to investigate your subconscious motivations. Feng shui can also be a mystery or a spiritual endeavor. You can think about feng shui as a magical force. See what happens if you imagine that everything is alive and in a constant state of evolution.

Chapter 1

Schools of Feng Shui

The origins of feng shui in China can be traced back more than 4,000 years, yet its roots extend further into antiquity to the practices of the earliest tribal healers. When the Earth originally formed, Mother Nature produced a variety of geographic regions. Some of these had ecological features that suited human inhabitants more than others. As spiritual leaders, the ancient Shamans were responsible for the health and success of the people. It was their role to read the landscape around them for features that would benefit the community. Throughout the ages, although its practices have become more sophisticated, the purpose of feng shui has remained essentially the same: to create environments that support well-being and prosperity.

It is believed that feng shui originated among Chinese farmers as a result of the development of agriculture, as they were no longer following a nomadic existence. The need for secure shelter and livelihood led to the realization of the importance of choosing the most favorable settings for homes and villages, where generations of families would enjoy good health, prosperous lives, and auspicious conditions. The farmers understood that if the land shielded their crops from the wind and provided fresh water, it would be fruitful and sustain them. Feng shui literally means "wind-water."

The ancient Shamans were visionaries who saw our planet as a living, breathing, conscious being and revered her. From closely observing the seasonal cycles of life that Earth offered, they began to understand the power of Nature's primary elements: fire, wood, water, earth, and metal. They honed skills to activate and direct the flow of the universal life force inherent in the landscape. Their traditions have continued through the ages and branched out into many forms, incorporating ancient wisdom with modern insights. One of these forms is the contemporary practice of feng shui, the art of placement originated by the ancient Chinese in order to create ideal building sites for their villages.

Because China is a vast land, with many distinct types of environments, various schools of feng shui arose over time. Individual practitioners incorporated local folklore, mystical beliefs, and even spells into the mixture of what they knew about the directions of the compass and the vital forces of the elements. Many of these ancient masters developed their own secret codes of practice. Their personal formulas, wisdom, and rituals were secretly guarded and passed on only from master to disciple.

In the modern world, we have therefore inherited numerous versions of feng shui, some of which may appear to contain contradictory guidance. Here, we are going to briefly explore the Form School, the Compass School, the Black Hat Sect, and Intuitive Feng Shui. Intuitive Feng Shui and the Black Hat Sect both combine the merits of the earlier schools with perspectives drawn from psychology, physiology, geography, landscaping, ecology, architectural design, the healing arts, medical science, interior design, artistry, folklore, and spirituality. *Exploring Feng Shui* thus blends ancient secrets and revelations with contemporary insight, knowledge, and techniques.

The Form School

The Form School, sometimes also known as Landscape Feng Shui, puts its primary emphasis on the contours of the natural environment, specifically its shape, size, elevation, and pattern of waterways. It focuses on the relationship between the surrounding land's formations and a dwelling, village site, or property.

The ancient Chinese noticed that life was easier and more prosperous when their homes were situated in sunny locations on southern sloping hills surrounded by larger hills that would break any harsh winds. To them the landscape resembled the shapes of sacred animals, some benevolent and protective and some threatening and aggressive. Animals symbolize the four cardinal directions in this tradition. The east is represented by a green dragon, the west by a white tiger, the south by a red phoenix, and the north by a black tortoise (see Figure 1.1).

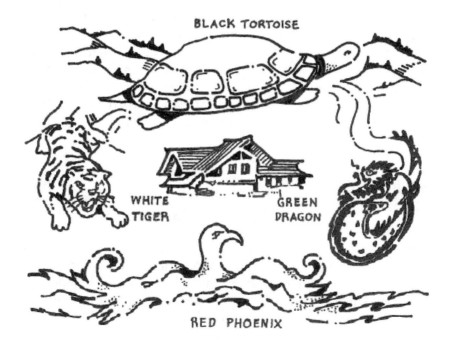

THE FORM SCHOOL

Figure 1.1. Landscape of hills and cardinal animals.

Contemporary practitioners of the Form School would suggest that an optimal location resembles a small comfortable armchair created by the natural terrain. It would include high-rolling eastern hills with lower-lying western hills. The dragon and tiger represent the arms. The tortoise-shaped hills in the north would form the high back of the chair. The low-lying phoenix-shaped hills to the south would form the seat of the chair. If there were a slow meandering river or water source in front of the location, it would create an ideal site.

A home or village in such a location would provide health, wealth, and happiness for all. There would be gentle breezes, fresh flowing water, and lush vegetation, which translated into abundant crops and herds. If the winds were too brisk or the water too swift, on the other hand, these could quickly sweep the beneficial life force and good fortune away. Villages nestled on hills had two important advantages: They were easier to defend from invading tribes and also spared their inhabitants from the frequent flooding in the lowlands.

The Form School is also concerned with sharp angles and long straight lines that can produce negative influences and adverse effects. Some landscapes propel energy in rapid and unhealthy patterns. Let us take a look at how a particular landscape and a corridor of fast chi affected one modern couple's marriage.

 # The story of Mary Beth and James

Mary Beth and James bought an adorable little house nestled among trees. Although the couple had a great deal of privacy, the trees were so close to the house that there was very little natural indoor light. Because they lived in the Pacific Northwest, where the weather is often overcast and rainy, it made the place seem a bit gloomy. They had been living there for about three months and were experiencing one problem after another with the house. First there was a leak in the roof that had to be repaired, then one of the toilets backed up, and then one of the main water lines broke. They were beside themselves. Because the money to make the repairs was adding up substantially, they began to argue a lot. But Mary Beth and James had gotten along so well before moving into this house. What could be wrong? They called me for a consultation, understandably worried about what might happen next.

To reach the house, you needed to drive down a long, narrow, sloping driveway that passed through a tunnel of tall trees and ended right at the front porch and door. There was almost no front yard. I surmised that the chi of the driveway was too strong and fast. It went directly into the house, where it was creating financial and emotional havoc. When I drove up, I also noticed that the gardens hadn't been attended for a long time. Along with the problem of overgrowth, there was a large stagnant pond filled with debris. Indeed, when I asked Mary Beth and James about the previous owners, they told me they had sold the house due to bankruptcy and divorce.

So what could my clients do to mitigate their situation? Fortunately, James was a good handyman. He was able to clean up the pond, install a pump to circulate the water, and placed six large fish in the pond. The flowing water in the pond would increase the flow of money into their lives. After a few weekends of hard work, the couple had the garden cleaned up. They found many beautiful plants that had been neglected and hidden under overgrown shrubbery! They purchased inexpensive ready-made fencing with an attractive arching gate to outline, enclose, and create a larger garden area in front of the house. They dug up ferns from the forest and used them to border the fencing and planted red impatiens to attract fortune and opportunity to their door.

I also suggested that the couple gather some stones to line the lower portion of the driveway, sending cars to a parking area on one side of the house. They used more stones to outline a path from the garden gate to the front porch. They hung a large wind chime from the corner of the house that was in a sight line with the long drive, and they placed a flagpole with a colored banner where the fenced garden and the driveway met. These remedies would slow the chi racing down the sloping driveway into their home.

As Mary Beth and James worked on their new home with the mutual intention of creating a more auspicious flow of energy, their relationship grew stronger. Their string of bad luck ended right away.

The Compass School

Over the years, feng shui masters began to acknowledge the influence of the metaphysical. Another school developed that took into consideration the forces of nature flowing from every direction of the compass. Knowledge of the power of these unseen forces became the most basic tool in the Compass School of feng shui.

It is well-known throughout the world that the Chinese invented the compass, although most people don't realize that its original purpose was to assist in locating burial grounds. The spirits of the ancestors were said to be able to assist living descendants. Therefore it was important to find the best place to bury and honor departed loved ones.

Practitioners of the Compass School invented a grid called the pakua (also translated from the Chinese by other traditions as the bagua) to divide a house or property into eight sectors. The bagua is derived from the *I Ching*, an ancient system of divination that predates both Taoism and Confucianism. Often considered the fountainhead of feng shui, the *I Ching*, also known as *The Book of Changes*, stresses the fundamental nature of transformation and flux in an individual's fortune and emphasizes the link between someone's destiny and the natural world. The sectors of the pakua correlate the various compass directions to aspects of life and qualities of chi, and each sector is governed by a symbol from the *I Ching*. In the Compass School, the pakua is always oriented to magnetic north.

The Compass School also incorporates Chinese astrology. Depending on your birth date in the Chinese calendar, which is different than the calendar used in the Western world, your life unfolds under the influence of a given sign, such as the rooster, ox, tiger, or rabbit. According to this system, you would need to emphasize different bagua zones in your home. It is a complicated although interesting means of evaluating personal energy and transformation. We will not go into this in any great detail in this book.

Figure 1.2. Pakua of the Compass School.

The Black Hat Sect

One of the most popular schools of feng shui in the Western world is the Black Hat Sect (BHS). Professor Thomas Lin Yun, Grand Master of the Black Hat Sect of Buddhism, developed this school in the 1980s as a hybrid of Tibetan Buddhism, Taoism, and feng shui, simplified for the average Westerner. BHS is based on a more spiritual approach than the Compass School, although this tradition also uses the bagua as one of its principle tools. It is widely practiced in the United States and is one of the main foundations of this book's exploration of feng shui.

In BHS, your property, your house, or an individual room is viewed from the position of its main entrance rather than magnetic north as in the Compass School. The bagua's octagonal shape encloses the yin/yang symbol, and its eight zones are spheres of influence governing the areas of life experience. They are associated with numerous components, such as colors, seasons, numbers, animals, and natural elements. BHS dictates specific remedies to enhance the energy of the different zones when they are out of balance. Many of these will be discussed in Chapter 5.

 Tanya's story

Tanya was a successful executive in an international hotel chain based in Chicago. When the firm needed to turn around a substandard hotel in Los Angeles, it made her a substantial offer and she relocated. But within four months of her arrival, her health began to deteriorate. She was hospitalized for several weeks with bleeding ulcers and heart palpitations. Then she went home to the Midwest to recuperate. In the familiar surroundings of the family farm among numerous brothers and sisters, she began to thrive. However, when she returned to her apartment in L.A., she became ill again.

Tanya and I are old friends, and I wanted to help her. Through our conversations it was clear that Tanya understood that to be able to thrive in L.A. she would need to create a setting reminiscent of her family home and garden, one that felt grounded, serene, and secure. Using the bagua, we located the zone of Family and Health in her garden, where she could grow organic vegetables. Tanya believed that whole foods were important for her health. They also stirred up strong and pleasant memories of home, hearth, and family.

Tanya's garden became a metaphor for healing her inner spirit as well as her body. She had always been interested in aromatherapy, and she began to grow healing herbs to add to lotions, oils, and soaps of her own creation. She became interested in healing stones and their meanings, subsequently placing them around her garden, paying particular attention to placing them in the Family and Health area of the bagua.

A whole new world began to grow from her ordeal. She created a small meditation area in her garden, and she found the solitude of gardening to be a blissful exercise in contemplation and mindfulness.

Slowly she became less anxious and fearful about her new life, which translated in her return to health and vitality. By emphasizing the bagua zone for healing, Tanya was able to pass peacefully through her "dark night of the soul."

Intuitive Feng Shui

Intuitive Feng Shui is distinguished from the more classical approaches by the practitioner's attention to gut instinct, feeling, symbolism, and intuitive wisdom. Rather than trying to analyze and interpret systems of energy or specific cultural ideologies from ancient times, the student and practitioner of Intuitive Feng Shui relies on his or her own discernment of what would enhance the balance of an environment.

What is intuition? It is your perceptions beyond the physical senses, which are available to assist you. It is the silent inner voice of knowing. It is your heart and spirit that inform your mind. It is your higher self, an aspect of the cosmic consciousness, speaking to your individual personality. It serves many purposes, only one of which is feng shui.

Interior designers, architects, Realtors, and many people in the healing arts acknowledge the relationship between the environment and health. They have adopted the practices of Intuitive Feng Shui in their businesses. The Intuitive Feng Shui practitioner bases his or her work on direct experience, knowledge, understanding, and intuition of the many ways that color, shape, texture, patterns, materials, and the architectural structure and placement of furniture can be adjusted to regulate the flow of energy.

The story of Joann and John

When you walk into the home of Joann and John, you enter a realm filled with serenity and oneness with the elements of nature. The couple would tell you that the creation of their home has been guided by their intuition. The central interior space is a tranquil garden atrium infused with the healing energy of flowing water, natural stone, light, and carefully chosen flowers, plants, and trees. It is a parklike oasis of rock waterfalls in a babbling pool, a slate pathway, and a simple stone bench. Abundant natural light filters through skylights, and prisms of colored light emanate from hanging cut glass and crystals that sparkle, dance, and kiss the image of a seated Kuan Yin. The goddess gracefully imbues the space with her loving energy.

Joann and John consciously choose furnishings, artwork, and building materials that have significance and meaning for them. Candles, incense, and spiritual icons amplify and enhance the life force of their home. Theirs is a setting beneficially enhanced by the techniques of Intuitive Feng Shui.

Chapter 2

Balance and Harmony

Y ou are on a path of emotional and spiritual growth throughout your life. Thus, one of the most subtle and profound struggles you may be facing is internal. You likely will be challenged whenever you seek to emerge into the fullness of your dreams instead of settling for your current reality. Even though it is natural to seek change and transformation, this process can seem a bit scary if you are worried about giving up a long-standing sense of identity and the comfortable parameters of your limitations. Nonetheless, you are going to be drawn, consciously or not, to what feeds your soul and gives you satisfaction and recognition in the physical world.

As children, we were more in tune with our soul selves. We had no problem hugging trees and talking to the butterflies. We surrendered to the joys of curling up and reading a book in the fort we built in the backyard or playing with the dollhouse we haphazardly, yet delightedly, created and decorated in the basement. We slept outside in sleeping bags, enchanted with the dark sky full of stars, and we could spend hours in the summer sun, happily splashing and running through sprinklers in the backyard. We lived in perfect harmony with Nature and our selves.

Then, as we grew older, we became busy with the responsibility of making our way in the world, forming and keeping relationships, and building careers to provide for those we love. Being busy usurped the innate ability to focus on our connections to both our inner and outer environments. Once the connective threads unraveled that joined us to the realm of the imagination and the oneness of all, so did our connections to the deeper levels of possibility in the world at large.

People use the idiom that they have "lost touch" with someone or something. Indeed. In time, we lose the ability to be touched, to be in touch, and to feel what can only be subtly touched, known, and felt. We lose touch with the balance of Nature and the harmony of being who we are. Yet our hunger for connection remains.

Feng shui is one way for you to heed the call of your soul, which is seducing you to return to a state of balance and harmony where you are open and available to life.

What is balance?

There is a great deal of talk these days about achieving balance in our lives. But what does that *really* mean? Some people think it means simplifying. Some people think it means not working so much and playing more. Working mothers think of balance in terms of spending more time with their young children. And although, yes, all these things may indeed contribute to a more balanced life, just what would that actually feel like? You may ask: How can I have a more balanced life? What do I have to *do*?

Well, the first order of business is to understand that balance is not only about *doing;* it is also about *being.* Most people believe that we must do something in order to bring about our being something or to create a better life for ourselves. Not quite. It actually works better (and faster) the other way around. If you are being something, then the doing naturally occurs. And that is where feng shui comes in.

The ancient secrets of feng shui can help you balance who you are being. Change is then inevitable. The fact that you have picked up this book means that you are already behaving in a new way. Who you are now being is an individual open to transforming your life and living more consciously.

When we feel balanced, we are living in a state of harmony. Feeling deeply connected to the natural world is fundamental to the sense of balance and well-being. Indeed, biologically, human beings are in partnership with the planet Earth. The idea that the Earth is a living organism in delicate balance is not new. Philosophers, Shamans, and sages of ancient civilizations from the Chinese to the Australian Bushmen to the Native Americans have always spoken of a world soul. Their cultures honor the circuitous flow of chi connecting humankind with the Earth, cosmos, and spiritual realms.

How does this translate into the contemporary world? Apart from the obvious need to live in a home that offers comfort and health—harmony—to the body, there is a deeper and age-old desire to dwell in a home that creates harmony for the mind and spirit. Feng shui takes this proclivity one step further by integrating areas of life experience and the elemental forces of Nature. The ancient Chinese sages, such as Fu Hsi and, years later, Confucius and Lao Tsu, noted that our responsibilities, identities, and life experiences could be combined within eight major areas, and specific forms of natural energy influence each of these areas. This observation is as valid now as it was in preceding eras.

In future chapters, we will cover the elemental forces of Nature and how they are reflected in your physical surroundings. For now, let's keep our focus on the different aspects of life experience.

Today, when we think of balancing our lives, most often we make a list of categories. We divide them into roles we play, such as being a mother, wife, husband, father, daughter, or son; and activities, such as being an athlete, provider, community volunteer, or student. Feng shui recognizes that these categories are important, and yet it views them as a reflection of the inner state of being. When we feel more in harmony within ourselves, we are able to balance our endeavors and the energy we bring to them.

Close your eyes and imagine your life and all its aspects. Try to see the whole; picture a circle with the areas divided up as slices of a pie. But remember, these are not really separate parts. What occurs in one area always affects the others. It is how you feel about these parts of your life and what you intend for them to be that is significant. Consider the following questions:

- Are you doing what you want in your life? Do you feel that you are on the correct path? Are you happy with your life's journey?
- Do you have time for stillness, quiet time for contemplation and looking within?
- Do you have a healthy and happy family life? Are you blessed with loving companionship and great relationships with your loved ones, partners, and friends? How much love is in your life?
- Do you feel a sense of gratitude for your ancestors, parents, and teachers?
- Are you experiencing fortune and good luck? Are opportunities for abundance offered to you?
- Do you feel good about who you are in your community? Are you known as a kind and loving person?
- Do you feel that you can express yourself? Do you have a voice to share your creativity?
- Do children and their happy laughter surround you? How happy is your own inner child? Does he or she have a creative outlet?
- Do you feel that you have a healthy, circuitous exchange of support with helpful friends and benefactors?
- Are you blessed with guidance from otherworldly beings—angels, saints, and deities?

In each moment you are deciding who you are and who you will become. So, who are you choosing to be? How much balance and harmony have you chosen for yourself?

Stillness as the source

Balance originates from practicing stillness. All the great wisdom traditions of the world teach that to find our essence and connect with the soul, to discover and experience the oneness of all, we must practice looking within. This process is often called contemplation, meditation, and, sometimes, prayer. For many people, the frequent and persistent demands of career, family, housework, children, and a social life make finding the space and time to be still problematic. But be still you must, because the soul self speaks most often and clearest in times of silence.

Basically, you can tap into a deep sense of knowing if you hold still long enough. In these moments, you are going to begin to hear a small voice inside that speaks straight from your heart and soul, a voice that is going to offer you guidance. Your core of inner knowingness is the source of balance and harmony—not the store-bought harmony found in the latest magazine articles, but the real one: an organic, authentic harmony.

So give yourself the gift of sitting for a few minutes every day and listening. As you practice, you can attune to the profound wisdom already present within you. Out of this practice can grow an abiding sense of trust and well-being that any personality prop, such as money, looks, or fame, could never give you. Feng shui can then help you align your surroundings to support the messages you receive.

Yin and yang

The Chinese concept of balance is a philosophy of polarities that are represented by yin and yang. Yin and yang are opposing forces from whose interaction and fluctuation the universe and its diverse forms emerge. They are often depicted as a tai chi circle of wholeness. Tai means the "supreme" and chi means the "ultimate." The yin-yang symbol itself expresses the interaction of these dual principles. For within each half of the circle, there is a small spot indicating that it contains a seed of the other.

Figure 2.1. The Chinese symbol of yin and yang.

The conjunction of these two opposing principles expresses the basic human experience. You cannot know yin without yang and vice versa. What is dark without light? What is softness without hardness? What is activity without rest? One quality in each polarity leads naturally back to the other. Every opposition can be mapped by yin and yang. Yin is feminine, yielding, and receptive. Yang is masculine, hard, and active. But we can also see the ultimate resolution of these forces in the balance of our surroundings.

Nature is the manifestation of divine balance. The moon is yin. The sun is yang. Yin is cool. Yang is hot. Feng shui attempts to duplicate organic balance in our human environments: our homes, offices, and communities. It aims to take maximum advantage of the currents of chi that circulate throughout the landscape by harnessing yin and yang attributes.

Simply put, balance can be established by your choice of furnishings, the art on your walls, and the shape and number of windows and doors. It is also found in the way you center and align objects on your tables. You have created balance any time opposites are paired in a room. Examples could include adding lighting to a dark room, placing soft furnishings among hard surfaces, and mixing masculine and feminine details.

Yin and yang landscapes

Yin signifies the shady northern side of a mountain. Yang signifies the sunny southern side of the mountain. They complete, complement, and interact with each other to create harmony in the natural world. Even though water is typically perceived as yin, a fountain or waterfall possesses both yin and yang energy because yang is active. Likewise, fire is typically perceived as yang, and yet the subtle glow of candlelight can create a nurturing and introspective yin ambiance.

In the landscape, yang energy is found in hills, mountains, and raised areas. Yin areas include valleys, rivers, and streams. A gently rolling countryside is considered a harmonious combination of the two. A flat stretch of land would be considered overwhelmingly yin, however, and a mountainous area, overwhelmingly yang.

In Chapter 3, we are going to look at how yin and yang are represented in the five elements.

Mixing yin and yang

As a beginner, you may not be able to identify whether a room is too yin or too yang. As previously noted, some rooms, depending on the activity for which they are used, should be predominantly yin or yang. For instance, your bedroom should be a predominantly yin room, suited to relaxing, sleeping, and reading. Your office should be a more yang space, suitable for meetings and decision-making.

Look around your room. Observe its shape, walls, windows, floors, furnishings, and decorations. Make a list of each yin and yang attribute. Assess the space in terms of its function and activity. Do not overdo either energy. Too much yang energy cannot be tolerated and displaces the yin energy, causing such an imbalance that in the end it can also lead to the loss of the yang energy. You would become drained.

The yin and yang of your environment

Balancing the yin and yang in your environment is the key to good feng shui. In general, the furnishing and decorations of your home and office should incorporate attributes of both. Only enhance one aspect more than the other when you intend to create a space that holds that energy for a purpose, such as a predominantly relaxing yin room for meditation or an active and lively yang recreation room.

Yin attributes include:

- **Shapes:** soft contours and curves, round or irregular shapes, low-level, and open.
- **Colors:** muted, pastels, and cool colors, such as green, blue, gray, or black.
- **Sensations:** sensuous, soft, relaxing, quiet, receptive, yielding, feminine, safety, loose, nurturing, comfortable, cozy, cool, peaceful, tranquil, and dark.
- **Objects:** pillows, flowers, plants, water features, and ceramics.
- **Activities:** resting, sleeping, meditating, reading, massage, and listening to relaxing music.

Yang attributes include:

- **Shapes:** rigid, upright, straight, long, tall, angles, narrow, and sharp.
- **Colors:** warm, bright colors, such as red, yellow, and gold.
- **Sensations:** hard, tight, hot, stimulating, lively, passionate, playful, noisy, active, simplicity, and precision.
- **Objects**: angular, pets, animal figurines, bright lights, TVs, and stereo equipment.
- **Activities:** action, parties, children playing, business meetings, and listening to upbeat music.

Consider the case of Jody. As an agent in the music industry, her job was to book and arrange the logistics of performances for her clients, who included many well-known classical musicians and singers. She had a small apartment in New York City, and her workspace was in her bedroom, making it more stimulating, or yang. Thus, when it was time to rest and relax, she had difficulty sleeping. If she was going to sleep there, her bedroom needed to be predominantly yin, much more nurturing and renewing.

With a little work, we were able to carve out a new workspace in her living room, which was already often a lively gathering center where her friends and clients could enjoy music, conversation, and dinner parties. The yang energy turned out to be more conducive to her work. Thus her bedroom became more yin, a nest where she could retreat for peace and rejuvenation.

 # The story of Tammi and Nick

Tammi and Nick were very much in love and had been dating for two years. Nick had the proverbial bachelor's pad, a loft apartment in Seattle where the walls were the original brick and mortar and the ceilings were high. Large windows looked out over Puget Sound. Nick's furnishings were an eclectic contemporary mixture, featuring combinations of chrome, glass, and leather. The surfaces were hard and the shapes angular and clean. He also collected contemporary art in bright bold colors. He had a state-of-the-art entertainment center with a large-screen TV and comprehensive music system. Nick's home was predominantly yang.

Tammi's houseboat was a cozy and rustic cabin. It was her little nest. The walls and ceiling were the original knotty pine. She liked her furnishings to be soft and cushy, the "shabby chic" look. She had cotton velvet slipcovers on her sofa and big armchair. She draped chenille throws over these among decorative down pillows made with tapestry fabrics and tassels. The colors she chose were deep hunter green and burgundy. She had inherited many of her grandmother's antiques, including round cherry wood coffee and end tables. Her home was predominantly yin.

Both Tammi and Nick loved their own homes and also loved spending time at each other's. Nick enjoyed the comfortable, relaxing, and cozy atmosphere of Tammi's houseboat, especially when he could feel it gently rocking on the water. Tammi loved the lively feel of Nick's place, especially when they would throw a party. Then it was "so much fun!" she would exclaim. She softened his rough edges. He lit up her world.

Soon they decided to take their relationship a step forward and move in together. It was a very exciting time and they looked forward to being a couple. But as they began to make plans, they realized that they were unsure of how to combine their respective homes and tastes. Each style was so distinctive. How could they balance the new environment to support each other and blend their personalities?

After a fair amount of thought and discussion, they decided that Tammi would move in with Nick because his space was larger. The two of them would have been too cramped in her little houseboat. They also each made a list of which items and furnishings they loved most or were especially meaningful. Nick's art and entertainment center were important to him. Tammi's heirlooms, comfy sofa, and chair were meaningful to her. They picked out new colors for slipcovers to complement and coordinate with his art. They bought a rug for the hardwood floors to match the furnishings. In this way, they were able to keep what they loved and balance the yin and yang of their new home together, as well as solidify their union.

The journey of the human spirit

Modern insight tells us that we need to live and work in healthy environments. Ancient wisdom recognizes that the healthiest places are as harmonious as Nature. In the same way that the natural world is constantly changing and cycling through seasons, the human spirit is constantly in process, changing, learning, and growing into new and different forms of balance. Thus, a home or an office is not only a physical place. It is also an emotional and spiritual vessel for a journey of discovery.

As you change, your task is to renew your balance. You will go "off balance" in order to grow. After you gain a sense of your new identity, you must seek to balance and secure that self. Once you feel stabilized again, you can take more steps "out of the box." Whenever you feel that life is out of balance, your soul is literally asking for attention. This can be frightening. But without the journey, balancing, shifting, and rebalancing, your life would be stagnant and full of frustration. To be true to your innermost self usually does mean making changes, large or small.

Every time you take a step in your life, the feng shui of your home is going to need to be realigned. To be healthy, our dwellings and workplaces must evolve, as we do, supporting us through our growth and transitions. Feng shui can help you become who you truly want to be. This is its secret power.

Let us take this journey now together.

Chapter 3

The 5 Elemental Forces of Creation

The 5 elements of chi

Chi, the universal life energy, can assume an endless variety of tangible forms. Whatever you can see, touch, taste, hear, or smell is an expression of chi. Even so, in ancient China, legendary sage and ruler Fu Hsi observed that everything in the world belongs to one of five basic categories. These are related to five elements found in nature: wood, fire, earth, metal, and water. Each element represents specific attributes of chi, such as color, shape, direction, and mood, and has numerous associations. They even correspond to the stages of life. Understanding the five elements is one of the most powerful tools of feng shui.

There are two essential ways of working with the five elements in your environment. The first and most basic approach is to balance them, for, as we observed in the last chapter, a balanced environment is harmonious and healthy and supports your intentions. Seeking a balance among the five elements can help you to pinpoint specific problems in your home or office that otherwise would be affecting you subtly, below your conscious awareness.

Way back when, Fu Hsi also noticed how the five elements indicate the interplay of chi within and between people and the environment. He found that these are dynamic forces that exert certain influences. Together they compose a continuous creative cycle, flowing one into the next. A preponderance of one element can also destroy or overpower another. Having the ability to recognize the relationships between the five elements puts you in charge of the flow of chi in your environment. Therefore the second approach is using this knowledge to initiate positive and life-affirming transformations.

Let us take a moment to consider the attributes of each of the five elements and some of their associations.

Wood

The wood element is associated with trees. The nature of a tree is at once connected to both the earth and the heavens. Its roots are firmly grounded in the earth and its branches reach towards the sky and heaven. Trees are considered sacred by many ancient and modern cultures. Wood can be pliant and bending like a willow, or strong and sturdy like an oak. When there is just the right amount of the wood element in an environment, the qualities of creativity, innovation, trust, flexibility, and cooperation are present. Wood relates to being social and active in the community.

On the negative side, when too much of the wood element is present, there can be a lack of creative flow, overexpansion, a sense of having too much going on, and the feeling of being overwhelmed.

Wood also represents the spring, new growth, and the color green. It is connected to the direction east, where the sun rises. In the life cycle, wood symbolizes babies and young children.

Qualities of the wood element are found in the following sources:

- ◆ Wood-building materials, such as wood floors, decking, paneling, and roof shingles.
- ◆ Wood furniture and furnishings, such as tables, chairs, cabinetry, armoires, and accessory objects.

- Trees, shrubs, plants, and flowers, both indoors and outdoors. Also man-made plants and flowers, such as those made from fabric and plastic.
- All-natural, plant-based, and organic materials and fabrics.
- Fabric and textiles with floral prints depicting leaves, plants, and flowers.
- Art that shows gardens, landscapes, flowers, and trees.
- Shapes that resemble trees, such as columns, beams, pedestals, and poles.
- The colors of the green spectrum, including teal, blue-greens, and aquamarine.

Fire

The fire element represents passion, energy, and enthusiasm. Fire is warming and is the element of the natural leader. In Chinese culture, fire is said to rule the eyes and intelligence because these show a person's inner light. It is connected to the direction south, for the sun. Therefore libraries, schools, and other creative and intellectual endeavors, as well as any manufacturing that utilizes fire, should be oriented towards the south under the element of fire. Fire also represents summer and the colors of the red spectrum. In the life cycle, fire symbolizes youth.

On the negative side, fire can be too hot and dangerous. When there is an overabundance of fire, it burns and can be destructive.

Qualities of the fire element are found in the following sources:

- Things that represent light and fire, such as fireplaces, candles, direct sunshine and abundant natural light, lighting elements, and electrical devices, such as TVs, stereos, and computers.
- Art, objects, and materials that represent the sun or fire.
- Art, objects, or materials that represent animals and people.
- Animals, either pets or wildlife.
- Things that are made from animals or look as if they are, such as leather, wool, feathers, fur, or textiles in animal prints.

- Shapes that suggest triangles, cones, and pyramids.
- The color spectrum of red, pink, and orange.

Earth

The earth element provides stability and grounding. Therefore it is related to legacies, land, and real estate. It also represents the qualities of patience, honesty, and being methodical. Earth is connected to the center of all the directions and, in the life cycle, the teenage years.

In the negative, when there is too much earth element present an environment can feel demanding, overly attentive, and suffocating.

You will find the properties of the earth element in the following sources:

- Earthenware objects, such as vases and pottery.
- Ceramic objects, such as tiles, tableware, and decorative pieces.
- Building materials made from stucco, adobe, brick, and earthen tile.
- Art, decorative fabrics, or textiles depicting a landscape, such as a southwestern desert or canyon, or a field of flowing wheat.
- Shapes such as squares and rectangles.
- The colors of the spectrum featuring yellows, cream, earth tones, and browns.

Metal

The metal element indicates business, prosperity, and financial success. Because metal symbolizes coins and rocks, one of the types of businesses that can benefit from the influence of this element is a jewelry shop. Hardware stores also fall under the category of metal. Buildings that house businesses that deal in money, such as banks and stock brokerages, are more likely to be successful when they are designed to include domes and arches because these represent the metal element.

Although the positive side of metal is success, the negative side can indicate conflict and be destructive, such as with a sword.

The color related to the metal element is usually white; however, it can also be silver or gold. Metal is connected to autumn and the direction west, for the setting sun. In the life cycle, it represents adulthood.

Qualities of the metal element are found in these sources:

- All types of metals, such as iron, chrome, steel, aluminum, stainless steel, copper, brass, silver, and gold.
- Stone surfaces for flooring, patios, and countertops, including marble, concrete, granite, flagstone, and river rock.
- All natural rocks, boulders, stones, and gemstones, including crystals and precious gems.
- Art pieces and sculpture made from or depicting metal or stone.
- Moving metal, such as clocks, mobiles, and wind chimes.
- The shape of the circle, ovals, roundness, and arches.
- The colors white, silver, gold, brass, and copper, as well as pastels.

Water

The water element represents learning, communication, and travel. It relates to literature and the arts. Many of the world's greatest cities of commerce are located next to water, such as Los Angeles, Hong Kong, New York, and London. Water can either be a gentle rain or a wild storm. The color of the water element is black. It is associated with winter and the direction north. In the life cycle, water represents old age.

Properties of the water element can be found in:

- Bodies of water of every kind, including swimming pools, ponds, fish tanks, fountains, and natural rivers, lakes, oceans, and streams.
- Objects and surfaces containing reflective glass, such as mirrors, cut glass, and cut crystal.
- Art that depicts the ocean, rain, or rivers and lakes.

- ◆   Shapes that are asymmetrical and free flowing.
- ◆   The black and midnight spectrum of colors, including gray, charcoal, and dark blue.

Balancing the 5 elements

Most of us can sense when something is out of order in an environment. This is intuitive. For instance, you would probably feel slightly uncomfortable and perhaps afraid walking alone along a cold, dark, and rainy street. Whereas lying in solitude on the green grass of a pretty, flower-strewn meadow in the sunshine would be a very pleasant and peaceful experience. In both instances you would be alone; however, your emotional response is likely to be completely opposite. So what is the difference?

We are all drawn instinctively to what feels comfortable and pleasant, and we prefer to withdraw from environments that feel uncomfortable and unsafe. In fact, on those occasions when we are confined or restricted to an environment that is uncomfortable, whether it is in the home or office, the drain of energy that occurs eventually takes its toll on our well-being and begins affecting other areas of our lives.

According to the feng shui tradition, people feel most comfortable in spaces that hold the five elements in balance. There the environment nourishes you and works in support of your creative intentions. When the five elements are out of balance, however, the environment can work against you. Too much water, for example, can sap you of energy, or internal fire.

      ## Caitie's story

Caitie asked me to come to her house for a feng shui consultation. She had an adorable sun-splashed cottage with wooden siding, inside and out. In her main living area were many French doors and windows that opened onto a private garden of green grass, trees, shrubs, and flowers. Caitie had placed a couple of tall, round, wooden architectural columns in her living room and installed several large ficus trees as well. She also had several pieces of rattan furniture that were covered in upholstery depicting Hawaiian botanicals. We determined that she had an overabundance of the wood element.

When I asked her how her daily life was going, Caitie described being overwhelmed. She felt scattered, as though she had too many projects going and couldn't finish or accomplish anything. Her ideas had become like a tangle of branches on an old apple tree that needed to be pruned. Feng shui teaches that once you balance the elements in your environment, what's going on in your life changes as well. There is an energetic correlation that is as mysterious as it is powerful.

Fortunately, Caitie's cottage had Mexican tile floors throughout, an attribute of the earth element. Her French doors and windows allowed natural light and sunshine to permeate the space, contributing the element of fire to the mix. All we needed to add were more metal and water elements to help balance the area.

In the weeks that followed, Caitie installed wrought-iron drapery rods over the windows and doors, and she painted the inside of the cottage white, thus introducing more of the metal element. To emphasize the water element, she replaced the coverings on some of her furniture with dark fabrics that had a watery motif, installed a small tabletop fountain, and hung a beautiful framed mirror over her fireplace. We also put a water fountain in her garden.

Little by little, in correlation with each addition and shift in the balance of the elements in her home, Caitie noticed her life changing. She found she was able to define the important projects she wanted to complete and to begin to make headway on each one. As a result she reported that she felt more in control of her life and her well-being.

You don't have to believe in feng shui for it to work its magic on your behalf the way it did for Caitie. You only need to follow the rules. These ancient secrets are astonishing and as relevant for our time as they were to Fu Hsi. After many years, I am still continuously amazed at the changes that occur when the five elements are in balance.

Evaluate the elements in your home

Before you go nuts trying to decipher the meaning of the five elements, I recommend that you do an evaluation to get an overall feeling of how well or poorly they are represented in your home. With pen and paper in hand, sit down in every room in turn. Start with the living room, for example. Take a moment to look around the room and then close your eyes. Do you notice how this room makes you feel? Open your eyes and jot down your observations and feelings on the paper.

Now create five columns on a sheet of paper. Label them for the five elements. Scan the room thoroughly and list every element that is present in the appropriate column. Take your time. The more detailed your observations are, the greater the ultimate benefits.

You might begin with the fire element. Referring back to the previous descriptions, look for any of the attributes that are associated with fire, such as the color spectrum of reds, oranges, and maroons. You may notice that there is red in the fabric of your curtains, pillows, or upholstery. Do you have any glass-topped tables? Are there red flowers in a cut crystal vase on an end table? Have you placed any candles around the room? These all represent the fire element. Continue working through the list of attributes for the fire element until you are sure you have exhausted all the possibilities.

The purpose of this simple exercise is to give you a feel for the balance of the five elements in your home. However, you can use this same method to evaluate your office or any other environment. In addition, as you scan your environment, remember that a wooden chair painted red incorporates both the fire element (the color red) and the wood element (the chair). Many objects and qualities in any space represent more than one element. So your rooms may be more balanced than you might initially perceive.

Next, evaluate the earth element. Any materials used in construction, such as ceramic tile floors or countertops or stucco walls, are attributes of earth. Do you have any old earthenware vases or pottery? Do you have indoor trees in clay pots? Are any of the objects in this room colored yellow, cream, taupe, or brown? For instance, are your curtains or your couch one of these colors? Is your furniture square or rectangular? Do you have clocks or lamps that are ceramic? Or a table with a tile top? Once you have studied the room thoroughly for characteristics of the earth element and made notes of what you have found, move on to the other elements: metal, wood, and water.

When you are sure that you have completely listed the sources of each element in every room, you may discover that one, two, or three elements predominate in your environment and the others have been almost entirely left out. Now you have an accurate assessment of what element is working and what element isn't working on your behalf.

Please remember to hang on to your notes, because you are going to need to refer back to them later in this chapter.

Attributes of the 5 elements				
Element: Wood	Fire	Earth	Metal	Water
Color: Green	Red	Yellow	White	Black
Shape: Columnar	Pointed	Flat	Arched	Irregular
Direction: East	South	Center	West	North
Creates: Fire	Earth	Metal	Water	Wood
Destroys: Earth	Metal	Water	Wood	Fire

The creative and destructive cycles of the elements

It is easy to recognize cycles in Nature, such as the progress of seasons and the daily course of the sun. You could say that at times elements of Nature are waxing like the moon, or gaining influence, and at other times they are waning, or losing influence. The energy of the elements is always in a state of becoming. The feng shui tradition recognizes the influence of the five elements as two opposite yet related tendencies: the Cycle of Creation and the Cycle of Destruction. Knowing which of the five elements can nourish or deplete another affords you an opportunity to harness them.

Figure 3.1. The Cycle of Creation.

The Cycle of Creation is productive and nourishing, just as it is in Nature. Looking at this cycle in terms of dynamic relationships, you can see that as one element becomes stronger, the preceding element lessens in force. Yet they are interdependent. No single element is strong in isolation. Another name for the Cycle of Creation is the Early Heaven arrangement.

As you can see in Figure 3.1, the cycle repeats itself endlessly. Wood sprouts, grows, and feeds fire, which consumes it and then produces ashes. Those ashes combine and become earth. Earth becomes strengthened only as fire wanes. Supplying the minerals that are the source of metal softens earth. Metal grows in power until it attracts water through condensation. Water gains strength and begins to flow freely. As water feeds and is absorbed by the growing power of wood, it becomes depleted in turn. Wood only loses impact as it is consumed

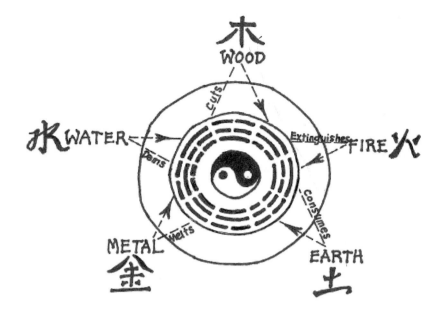

Figure 3.2. The Cycle of Destruction.

within the flames of fire. Finally, as fire burns out, its remnants strengthen and solidify into earth, bringing us full circle.

The Cycle of Destruction is also known as the Cycle of Conquest or the Latter Heaven. It represents the ways that the elements can overpower, control, and compete with one another. Starting at the top of Figure 3.2, you can see that wood, by drawing nourishment and energy through its roots, depletes earth. In turn, earth overpowers water, just as a dam controls a river. Water douses and thereby extinguishes fire. Fire overpowers metal by melting it. Completing the Cycle of Destruction, metal dominates wood, just as the sharp blade of an ax or a saw can cut through a tree trunk.

Once you are aware of the creative and destructive cycles, you can more easily cultivate a balance among the five elements in your home. Use them to enhance an underrepresented element and minimize the impact of a dominant element.

Enhancing an element in your home

Return now to the notes you made during your evaluation exercise a few pages back. From these, it should be apparent where there are excesses and deficits of specific elements in each room. Please take this opportunity to consider ways to strengthen the representation of elements that are lacking. If you can only make one change for now, focus on this balancing technique as your first step.

In order to enhance an element in a given room, not only can you add objects that are the source of the element itself, you can also introduce objects to the room that hold attributes of the preceding element that nourishes it from the Cycle of Creation:

- To enhance and balance wood, introduce wood and highlight with water.
- To enhance and balance fire, introduce fire and highlight with wood.
- To enhance and balance earth, introduce earth and highlight with fire.
- To enhance and balance metal, introduce metal and highlight with earth.
- To enhance and balance water, introduce water and highlight with metal.

For a final touch, remove or avoid placing items related to the controlling element from the Cycle of Destruction in that same area of your home. Those would be counterproductive. When you are ready for the next step, try the next balancing technique.

10 quick and easy ways to enhance the 5 elements in any room

Remember to keep each element in balance with the others.

1. A bouquet of red roses introduces both fire (the color red) and wood (the flowers).
2. A healthy indoor plant in a black pot incorporates both wood (the plant) and water (the color black).
3. A zebra or leopard print throw and pillows on a chair, bed, or couch add fire.
4. An arrangement of white candles in cut glass candlesticks brings in fire (the candles), metal (the color white), and water (the glass).
5. A bowl of goldfish holds several elements: water (the glass bowl and the water), metal (the color gold), and fire (the fish).
6. A painting of a desert landscape framed in wood introduces wood (the frame) and earth (the landscape).
7. A tabletop fountain with splashing water brings in the water element.
8. A chrome wind chime with a wooden clapper adds both metal (the chrome) and wood (the wooden clapper).
9. Ceramic tableware painted in yellows and blues introduces both earth (the pottery and the color yellow) and water (the color blue).
10. Painting the walls of a room in yellow and cream tones, and draping your windows with curtains to match, adds the earth element.

Reducing a dominant element in your home

In order to balance the impact of a dominant element in a given room, match that element with its controlling partner from the Cycle of Destruction. In addition, you can refine the balance by highlighting the area with the qualities of the two subsequent elements from the Cycle of Creation that the dominant element nourishes:

+ When wood predominates, introduce metal. Highlight the room with qualities of fire and earth.
+ When fire predominates, introduce water. Highlight the room with qualities of earth and metal.

- ◆ When earth predominates, introduce wood. Highlight the room with qualities of metal and water.
- ◆ When metal predominates, introduce fire. Highlight the room with qualities of water and wood.
- ◆ When water predominates, introduce earth. Highlight the room with qualities of wood and fire.

 Brian's story

Brian was a manufacturer's representative for a sportswear company that specialized in beach and surfing attire. Even though he was already a successful fellow at age 29 and had been able to buy an attractive condominium, he felt that he could be doing a lot better financially. His personal goals were to earn more money and improve his standing in the industry. He was an avid snowboarder, skateboarder, and surfer who had won numerous skateboarding championships in his younger years. He dreamed of parlaying his name as a champion into the creation of his own thriving sportswear line targeted to boarding sports of all kinds.

Brian ran his business from a home office located in one of the bedrooms of his condominium, which was where we met one afternoon for a consultation. As I looked around, I immediately noticed an overabundance of the metal and fire elements. The office was furnished with metal filing cabinets and a chrome-and-glass-topped desk, as well as wrought-iron lamp bases and curtain rods. In addition, he was overusing the color red in the fabric of his chair and the curtains, the room was exposed to a lot of direct sunlight, and he possessed an enormous amount of electronic equipment. Specifically, he had two computers (a laptop for business and another for playing computer games), stereo equipment and a DVD player, a large screen TV, a Palm Pilot, and assorted handheld electronic games.

Brian shared that lately he had been experiencing a problem with his temper. He would sometimes "lose his cool" with the manufacturers who employed him and his customers, a tendency that was beginning to cause conflicts on the job. We discussed how an overabundance of fire energy could make a situation "too hot" and an overabundance of metal energy could be "cutting" like a knife. He asked me to help him remedy this unhealthy pattern with feng shui techniques.

We agreed that the five elements in Brian's office were interacting in a destructive pattern. Because fire was already balancing a preponderance of metal, we merely needed to reduce the amount of metal in the room and highlight with attributes of water and wood. Then, to reduce and balance the fire element, we needed to emphasize the water element and highlight the room with attributes of the earth element.

We began our task by cleaning out some of the electronic equipment in Brian's office, leaving only what was necessary to get his job done. By removing the extra devices, he found he could be more focused on business. He wasn't as distracted by music, TV, and games. We also took out the red curtains and hung wooden shutters to reduce the amount of natural light in the room and to add more of the wood element. Next Brian replaced his chrome-and-glass-topped desk with a wooden desk. To introduce the earth element we added ceramic lamp bases and highlighted the room with antique-looking pottery.

Lastly, it was essential to introduce the water element. Brian decided to go "all out" and installed a large saltwater aquarium inhabited by gorgeous fish of many colors, shapes, and species. On a joint shopping excursion we found a lovely framed painting that he adored depicting the Santa Barbara coastline and Pacific Ocean.

Throughout the process, which took several weeks, Brian became more organized and less cluttered. He took greater pride in his attractive office space and also felt better about himself and his work. As a result, business started picking up effortlessly and he felt "cooler" in every sense of the word. His bosses and clients were treating him with respect and admiration, and he was no longer acting impatiently or angrily. Brian started to put together a practical business plan outlining his dream sportswear line. Soon he felt confident enough to talk about it with his friends and family. A few months later, he had already located a potential source of funding for his new company.

◆ ◆ ◆

You can work with the secret of the five elements to achieve success and emotional balance in the same way that Brian did. Think of it as a favorite family recipe handed down and refined for generations. Now that you have the recipe you can practice seasoning it according to your own taste. There is plenty of room for self-expression. I encourage you to be imaginative and playful as you explore balancing.

Chapter 4

Mapping Your Environment

In the preceding chapters, you have learned about the importance of balance in the creation of healthy chi. You have seen how the five elements in your home or office mirror qualities of your life and can be harnessed to transform them. Let us now explore together how feng shui can be used to support your heartfelt intentions on a deeper level. What else can you do to bring more love, joy, and abundance into your life?

The bagua

The bagua is an octagonal template or grid used in the practice of feng shui to map every environment. It is borrowed from the *I Ching*, also known as *The Book of Changes*, which is an ancient Chinese divination system and guide to right action. *Ba* means "eight" and *gua* means "trigram." In the *I Ching*, a trigram is a symbol made up of a set of three lines, either broken or unbroken, representing the trinity of heaven, Earth, and humankind. Each trigram represents a distinct way that yin and yang combine in Nature to create chi.

In feng shui, each of the zones (guas) of the bagua corresponds with one of eight specific areas of life experience. When you overlay the bagua on a plot of land, a building, a garden, a floor plan, a single room, or even a desktop, it becomes possible to identify these zones, analyze them, and improve the flow of chi. The eight zones of the bagua represent the following aspects of life experience: Journey and Career, Self-Wisdom and Knowledge, Family and Health, Prosperity and Abundance, Fame and Reputation, Marriage and Relationship, Children and Creativity, and Helpful Friends and Travel. In addition to their correspondences with various *I Ching* trigrams and their meanings, these life zones are influenced by certain elements and colors and correlate with the directions of the compass.

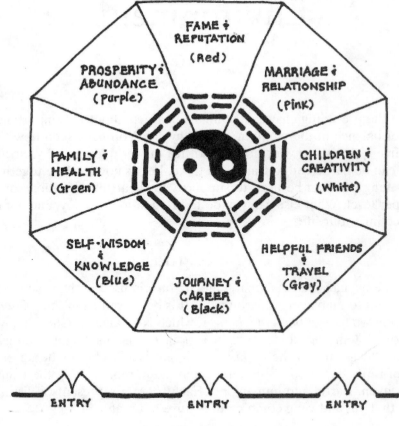

Figure 4.1. The bagua map.

How to use the bagua

Draw a floor plan

The easiest way to begin using the bagua is to draw a floor plan of your home. You could also choose to begin working in your office, your bedroom, or your garden, and that's perfectly acceptable. But no matter where you start out, you are going to need a clear diagram of your home, office, or room, representing its shape and approximate dimensions. Please don't worry that you are not a brilliant artist; no one needs see your drawing but you. You can use graph paper to help you draw the floor plan as accurately as possible.

Next, trace the illustration of the bagua map from page 58 on tracing paper. An idea that could make this process simpler is then to take your tracing to a copy shop and have it enlarged. (You might want to trace it on tracing paper again afterwards.) You are going to lay the bagua on top of your floor plan.

Identify the mouth of chi

In order to orient the bagua, you must first locate what is called the "mouth of chi." The mouth of chi is where chi flows into your home or a given room. Not all schools of feng shui apply the same method for orienting the bagua. Some are strict about using the compass directions. However, I advocate aligning the main front door of your house, no matter which door you use most frequently, with one of the following bagua zones: Self-Wisdom and Knowledge, Journey and Career, or Helpful Friends and Travel.

Observe. When you are standing in front of your house, is the front door on the left-hand side, in the middle, or on the right-hand side? The left-hand side puts it in the area of Self-Wisdom and Knowledge. The middle locates it in the area of Journey and Career. It falls in the area of Helpful Friends and Travel when it is on the right-hand side.

You would apply the same orientation method when working on the feng shui of a single room. Please note: The mouth of chi of every room in your house could correspond with a different compass point. That is to be expected. This means that even though the front entrance, or mouth of chi, to your overall home may lie in the north, the mouth of chi to a particular room, such as your kitchen or bedroom, could lie in a different direction.

Once you have superimposed the bagua over your floor plan and properly aligned the mouth of chi, it becomes possible to study where the different parts of your home fall within the bagua template. Now you are ready.

The 8 bagua zones

In order to implement the bagua as a mapping device, it is important to understand the unique qualities and influences of each of its zones. These are some of the many ways the bagua can be used to guide your life and realize your dreams.

Journey and Career

*"The longest journey is the journey inwards
of him who has chosen his destiny."*

—Dag Hammarskjold

Ever-flowing and moving, water is the element of Nature associated with the area of the bagua called Journey and Career. This section is ruled by the *I Ching* trigram K'an, which translates as "water" and is symbolic of the flow of life. It is located directly in the center of the bottom of the bagua, or the north. Black is its color.

This area generates the chi that activates your career, whether you currently work as a corporate executive, a stay-at-home mom, or a volunteer. However, it represents more than your job alone. It represents your journey. Your life resembles a trip down a river. Sometimes the river is swift and sure. Other times you must maneuver through difficult rapids. The flow can also seem as slow as though you were sailing and hit the doldrums.

Most of us do not feel fulfilled without a sense of purpose. Your life's journey has an outer purpose and an inner purpose. The outer purpose concerns goals, destinations, and achieving this or that. The inner purpose concerns a deepening of your true self. Your outer journey may contain thousands of steps. Your inner journey has only one. Although you may often feel as if your progress is aimless, it is important to gain a clear idea of what you want your journey to be, where you want it to go, and what life experiences you want to embrace. Balance in life begins by making choices about your life's work and the contribution you want to make.

Enhance the Journey and Career zone of the bagua when:

- You are looking for a new job.
- You are planning to change careers.
- You would like your work to go more smoothly.
- You are seeking a higher-profile position.
- You are going through a midlife crisis.
- You would like to reinvent yourself.
- You are about to do something new and different.

The Journey and Career zone is a natural place to include objects that depict or incorporate water in some fashion. You could decorate it with paintings or photographs of oceans, seas, lakes, and ponds, or install a fountain, aquarium, or waterfall. Consider how you might use objects made of cut glass. If this area overlays the entrance to your home, you may choose to hang a crystal chandelier in this location. Because the color that corresponds to this zone is black, you could paint the front door black. In other kinds of rooms, you could utilize black objects to enhance the chi in this area.

You can activate and strengthen the chi in this area by placing objects there that relate to your career or expertise. If you were in the banking business, for example, you might place a dish of coins in this area to symbolize money. If you were an opera singer, you might put a music box or an instrument here.

Self-Wisdom and Knowledge

"This above all: to thine own self be true, and it shall follow, as the night the day—thou canst not then be false to any man."
— William Shakespeare, *Hamlet*

The *I Ching* trigram Ken, which translates as "mountain," rules the zone of Self-Wisdom and Knowledge. This area is located on the lower left-hand corner of the bagua, or the northeast. Blue is its color.

This zone represents a cave of quiet self-inquiry and introspection located within your body when you are as still as a mountain and burrowing inward. It generates the chi that supports disciplines and practices contributing to personal growth, such as self-inquiry, meditation, contemplation, prayer, or yoga. It represents inspiration, fresh ideas, and education, both in the form of scholarly learning and of non-traditional courses of study.

You must cultivate the inner world to balance the outer world. When you can sustain a regular practice that supports your inner life, the rest of your life is stabilized.

Enhance the Self-Wisdom and Knowledge zone of the bagua when:

- You are in counseling.
- You are studying, whether for a degree or your own self-edification.
- You want to foster self-empowerment.
- You are practicing yoga.
- You want a sanctuary for meditation or prayer.
- You need a more peaceful mind or lifestyle.

The Self-Wisdom and Knowledge zone is the ideal location for a study, den, or meditation room, or the perfect corner in a room for a home altar. To activate the chi in this area, place objects or items there that symbolize your personal spiritual practice, such as prayer beads and prayer books or your library of books or tapes on self-growth and other subjects that you are studying. The art here could depict meditations and pictures of spiritual teachers, such as Jesus, Buddha, Mother Teresa, or Mohammed.

Pictures of majestic mountain peaks can also strengthen this area of the bagua. Because the color blue is associated with it, if the entrance to your home is overlaid by this gua, you might consider adding an area rug in shades of blue or placing a blue vase full of fresh flowers on the hall table.

Family and Health

> *"A wise man should consider that health is the greatest of human blessings, and learn how by his own thoughts to derive benefits from his illnesses."*
>
> —Hippocrates

The bagua zone called Family and Health is ruled by the *I Ching* trigram Chen, which translates as "thunder." Thunder is symbolic of the voice of your ancestors, elders, teachers, and also of your descendants and other relatives. The Chinese believe that when the spirits of our ancestors are happy, it results in blessings and fortune. This zone is located in the middle of the left-hand side of the bagua, or the east. The wood element governs this area. Green is its color.

Taking care of your family relationships, as well as your physical health, is of utmost importance. Family may include your biological family, as well as your close friends, coworkers, and members of any other close-knit groups in which you are involved. Family and friends are the foundation of health and endurance, especially in times of challenge. When this zone is in balance you should attract more positive experiences.

Enhance the Family and Health zone of the bagua when:

- You are planning surgery (or someone in your family is).
- You are ill or recovering from illness (or someone in your family is).
- You want to foster the love and support of friends and family.
- You want to heal a rift with a friend or family member.
- You want to resolve a family crisis.
- You are going through a divorce.
- You are getting married.
- You participate in sports and fitness activities.

The Family and Health zone is a natural place to include objects that depict or incorporate wood, plants with rounded leaves, and flowers. Floral prints in fabrics, landscape paintings and photographs, and fresh flowers would all be appropriate touches. Because the color green is associated with this zone, you could place a green candle, a green bowl, or a green vase here. Or you could furnish it with something painted green, such as a table or chair, or sofa pillows in a floral fabric.

When a family member or friend is ill or preparing for surgery, an ideal way to enhance this area is by creating an altar or a poster collage depicting that individual in healthy times. Include pictures, mementos, and affirmations embodying health and fitness. Place green or blue candles and fresh flowers on the altar.

My Family and Health zone overlays the main bathroom in my house. The walls are painted peach and complemented with green towels and a green rug. On one wall I have hung a gorgeous print of Monet's *Irises*, which depicts a blooming garden. A rustic green wooden cabinet displaying soaps, lotions, candles, and essential oils hangs over the commode. The mirror is framed in wood stained with an antique wash in a soft green tone. I frequently affix affirmations, inspirational quotes, and other "thoughts for the day" to it.

Prosperity and Abundance

> *"Affluence, unboundedness, and abundance*
> *are our natural state."*
> —Deepak Chopra, *Seven Spiritual Laws of Success*

The *I Ching* trigram Sun, translated as "wind," rules the zone known as Prosperity and Abundance. Wind is symbolic of the constant and steady flow of blessings and good fortune. This area is located in the upper left-hand corner of the bagua, or the southeast. The water element governs this area. Purple is its color.

Prosperity is a quality that most people naturally associate with income. However, it can actually pertain to anything that you find intrinsically valuable, such as family, friendships, power, money, or health. This area governs the finances and material things in life, but with an emphasis on the gradual and steady accumulation of wealth and other forms of abundance. Abundance that is reliable provides security and harmony to an individual or a family.

Enhance the Prosperity and Abundance zone of the bagua when:

- You want to earn more money.
- You are financially struggling, facing debt, or bankruptcy.
- You wish to accumulate resources.
- You are making new investments.
- You would like greater abundance in any area of your life.

- You have a general feeling of not-enough.
- You want to acknowledge your blessings.

You can activate and strengthen the chi of the Prosperity and Abundance zone by using water features, such as fountains and aquariums. Water symbolizes the positive flow both of chi and of cash. But because of the dynamics of flow, water features with moving water are more desirable than standing pools of water. Another way to stimulate the chi is by placing representations there of what you consider valuable, such as Monopoly money, photographs of friends, and magazine advertisements depicting material wealth or circumstances you would like to attract. You can also enhance the area with purple, blue, and red accessories, wall hangings, flowers, and fabrics.

It is always a good idea to enhance the Prosperity and Abundance zone with your collectibles. They could increase in value. My client Rick is an expert in collectibles. For many years he and his wife have lived in the same house, where he maintains a small office and a storage room to pursue this interest. Ironically, these rooms are located in the Prosperity and Abundance zone of the house. Over the years, Rick slowly and steadily created a prosperous nest egg in his spare time. He was able to retire at a young age after having built a solid financial foundation around stamps and coins.

Fame and Reputation

*"Imagine the you that you would be if you lived the highest
thought of yourself every day."*
—Neale Donald Walsch, *Conversations with God*

The zone of Fame and Reputation is associated with Li, the *I Ching* trigram that means "fire." Because the fire in this area pertains to a person's inner light, it is sometimes referred to as the "house of illumination." The fire also signifies the trust, integrity, and reliability that are required for a positive reputation. This zone is located in the center of the top of the grid, or the south. Red is its color.

The Fame and Reputation zone relates to your standing in your community, your social sphere, and your business circles. It also represents self-esteem, confidence, and integrity. A positive reputation is auspicious. It can attract opportunity and good fortune, for when you are well regarded, people want to invest in you and be around your positive influence. In a very real sense, this is your fame, even if it is only on a local level.

The trigram Li teaches us to be mindful of what we become famous for doing, being, or having, because whatever it is will adhere to us for a very long time. Your reputation says who you are in your community and in the world. It either contributes towards or detracts from your life's foundation of balance and harmony.

Enhance the Fame and Reputation zone of the bagua when:

+ You want to bolster your business reputation within your company or industry.
+ You want to increase your positive influence in philanthropic organizations, politics, your community, or the arts.
+ You want more recognition from your friends and family.
+ You want to gain notoriety.
+ You have low self-esteem.

Activate and strengthen the chi of this gua by displaying any of your awards, trophies, or certificates of achievement. Consider a symbolic object, art piece, or accessory that brings to your own mind your sense of fame and reputation. Because the fire element rules this area of the bagua, utilize enhancements that symbolize fire, such as candles, lighting, and electronic equipment, as well as anything depicting animals. You could include animal prints and pictures of animals to activate this chi; think the "safari look." Remember also that you can include the entire spectrum of the color red. Consider decorating here with red candles, red fabrics, and red flowers.

Marriage and Relationship

"Relationship is surely the mirror in which you discover yourself."
—Krishnamurti

Earth represents the receptive, ever-embracing principle of unconditional love. Therefore the zone of Marriage and Relationship relates to the *I Ching* trigram K'un, which translates as "earth." The receptive earth teaches us to receive love openly. It is in loving honestly that we learn to express love unconditionally. This section is located in the upper right-hand corner of the bagua, or the southwest. Pink is its color.

This zone governs all love relationships, including marriage, dates, partnerships, and non-traditional unions. On a spiritual level, it also represents your relationship with yourself. In order to love another, you must learn to love yourself. The trigram K'un is the most yin, or feminine, of the trigrams. The lessons it holds are about trust, unconditional love, and the supportive partnership of a loving couple.

Enhance the Marriage and Relationship zone of the bagua when:

- ◆ You are getting married.
- ◆ You want to improve your current love relationship.
- ◆ You have been unlucky in love.
- ◆ You want to nurture and enrich yourself.
- ◆ You want to attract a new lover or spouse.
- ◆ You are forming a business partnership.

If you have been unlucky in love, boosting the chi in this zone of the bagua in your home and office can jumpstart your romantic life. Use attributes of the earth element to activate and strengthen the chi of this area, such as pottery, earthenware vases, and ceramic accessories. Select objects for the Marriage and Relationship zone that are colored red, pink, and white.

Think in terms of pairs. Two of a kind of anything will do, whether they are two red heart pillows or two ceramic candlesticks holding pink candles. Choose artwork that depicts romance and love, such as paired figurines, a sculpture or a picture of a loving couple, or two ceramic lovebirds. I have a friend, a writer, whose desk happens to be placed in the Marriage and Relationship zone of her living room. She works at home and cannot move it. But that's okay because, in fact, she would like to find a husband with whom she can collaborate on her projects. Above her desk she has placed a painting of a couple from Egyptian mythology. She also took down a medieval poster of a unicorn tapestry because that is a symbol of chastity. I advised her to remove images of women alone or groups of women only, because single women frequently don't realize that these are reinforcing that energy.

Children and Creativity

*"Our creative dreams and yearnings come from a divine source.
As we move towards our dreams, we move towards our divinity."*
—Julia Cameron, *The Artist's Way*

The *I Ching* trigram that rules the zone of Children and Creativity is Tui, which means "lake." A lake represents creative life born from a deep stillness. This area is located in the center on the right-hand side of the bagua, or the west. The metal element governs it. White is its color.

This zone influences the chi relating to fertility, children, and creativity. It encourages the flowering of imagination within our children and us. You especially want this area to be uplifting and well managed if you have children in your house. It also pertains to the fostering and expression of new ideas and to inspiring the artist and inner child.

Enhance the Children and Creativity zone of the bagua when:

- You want to become pregnant.
- You want to bring out your own inner child.
- You want to improve your parenting skills.
- You want to nurture your children's creativity.
- You want to encourage your creativity.
- You are taking art classes.
- You are a professional artist of any kind—a singer, a dancer, a writer—or are aiming to be one.

The Children and Creativity zone of the bagua corresponds to the metal element. Therefore you can bring in the color white, round and oval shapes, metal sculptures, and stones to enhance its chi. Handmade objects and artwork that you or your children have made are good enhancements for this area, as well as photographs of children and babies. Any windowsill, nook, or shelf can be used to display a child's artistic endeavors. It is important, I think, to surround yourself with these reminders of happy, playful moments. These images affirm the positive emotions that you want to integrate into your household and reinforce messages of support and encouragement.

My kitchen is in the Children and Creativity zone of my home's bagua. I've always thought that this is an auspicious place for it, because cooking is a nurturing and creative act, and also because this room contains the abundant energy of children running in and out. When my two sons were in elementary school, they enjoyed making pottery. One summer, the younger one took a pottery class in which the instructor gave him plenty of one-on-one attention. They threw pots and worked on the pottery wheel. The results were many wonderful bowls, plates, and small containers to hold jewelry and other treasures or to place a candle. During the holidays, we would also go to stores where you can paint already-made figurines or dishes and have them fired. Many of the items my boys made are displayed in my kitchen. In addition, I purchased a set of refrigerator magnets of inspirational words, which can be arranged and rearranged into clever sentences. We also use the refrigerator as a site to post artwork, affirmations, and quotations.

Helpful Friends and Travel

"Without friends no one would choose to live,
though he had all other goods."

—Aristotle

The area of Helpful Friends and Travel is ruled by the *I Ching* trigram Ch'ien. Ch'ien translates as "heaven" and is the symbol of the Divine manifested through humanity. It is located in the lower right-hand corner of the bagua, or the northwest. Gray is its color.

Helpful friends are those people we sometimes call "Earth angels" who support us along our life's journey. They are the mentors and benefactors who help us make our dreams come true. In business and the theater world, investors are even called "angels." There is a notion that heavenly beings may be secretly sent to Earth disguised as beneficial people. Perhaps you can recall a time you told someone, "You must be heaven sent!"

The other aspect of this zone is Travel. It governs anything related to travel, including family vacations, business trips, and romantic getaways. When we are traveling we oftentimes need assistance. As Blanche Dubois said in *A Streetcar Named Desire*, "I have always depended on the kindness of strangers." By activating the chi in this area, you could receive help from unexpected sources or win vacation trips and cruises.

Enhance the Helpful Friends and Travel zone of the bagua when:

- ◆ You want to attract more helpful people, such as mentors, contacts, and benefactors.

- ◆ You want to increase your customer database and stimulate referrals.

- ◆ You would like to travel more often.

- ◆ You are setting out on a trip.

- ◆ You would like to experience more synchronicity in your life.

- ◆ You want to attract the spiritual guidance of angels, saints, or living masters with whom you feel a connection.

To activate the energy of intercession, enhance this area of the bagua with pictures of spiritual masters from whom you would like to seek assistance. It is good to place books about the lives of saints, spiritual masters, and teachers here to summon spiritual intervention and practical help. Remember to ask!

You can also place pictures in this zone of travel destinations representing the adventures you would like to experience. This is one of the ways that you can anchor an intention for a trip. Use objects and furnishings here that are in shades of gray, white, and black in charcoal and silver tones.

Odd-shaped floor plans

Modern houses and apartments can be oddly shaped. Rooms take many unusual shapes, as well. When overlaying the bagua template on a room or home, we often discover that a whole zone of the bagua is missing or indented, and sometimes we find, conversely, that a zone is projected or enlarged. Projections strengthen the qualities of the particular zone, whereas an indentation weakens it. Your floor plan and bagua overlay could hold very important clues about why certain aspects of your life are working for you or against you.

Let's consider the case of Maureen. Maureen had divorced her husband six years before I met her. After about three years she was ready for another long-term relationship. She also wanted to have children, which was something she and her husband never got around

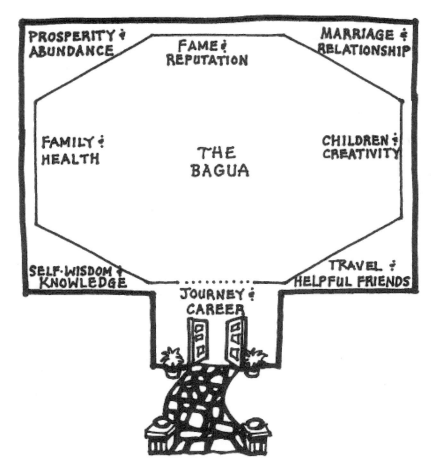

Figure 4.2. Projection of Journey and Career zone.

to doing. She was a beautiful woman with a great figure and outgoing personality who was friendly, smart, and accomplished. Yet no matter how many potential partners she dated, none of them seemed to pan out. Usually when Maureen had a goal in mind she was relentless until it was accomplished. And now, at 39, she wanted marriage and a family before her biological clock wound down!

Frustrated and longing for intimacy, Maureen called upon me to assess the feng shui of her little cottage. This would be a simple consultation, as she was specifically interested in this one area of her life. She told me that everything else was balanced and harmonious. I explained how feng shui teaches us about the unseen forces in our lives that affect us through the environment, even when we are unaware of them. Many times we unconsciously repeat long-standing patterns when we select the structure of the homes in which we live.

After seeing how the bagua overlay Maureen's home and talking with her about her past homes, we discovered that she had consistently chosen homes that were missing the zone of Marriage and Relationship. It had been true of the home she lived in before her marriage had broken apart. Now the floor plan of her cottage reflected the same missing zone, as you can see in Figure 4.3. Maureen's life was repeating a pattern that she had set into place for many years without realizing it.

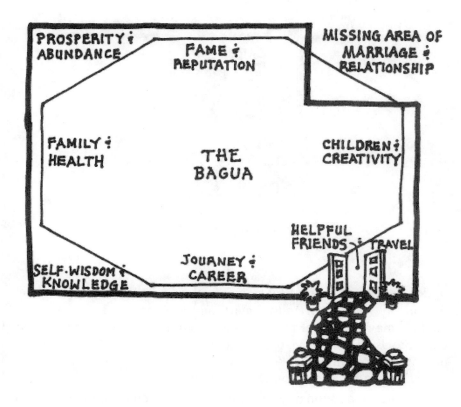

Figure 4.3. Missing zone of Marriage and Relationship.

Please do not worry unduly about missing zones. Just regard them as clues about the patterns of energy you may need to address. In the next chapter, we are going to learn about remedies for the most common problems in the bagua. There are many feng shui "cures" available to infuse your home and your life with beneficial chi energy, even when you have an irregular floor plan.

The magic unfolds

When you first started this chapter, you may have believed that only one or two areas of your life needed enhancing, right? Now I am betting that you have found ideas for improvements in every zone of the bagua. After all, isn't your goal to create overall balance and achieve a harmonious, loving, joyful, and abundant life?

Please allow me to make a suggestion. Although balance throughout the bagua does result in greater happiness and comfort, it is usually better to address only one or two areas of the bagua at a time. Consider which zones display the most pressing need for attention. Perhaps these are Fame and Reputation and Marriage and Relationship. Focus on these first. Otherwise you may dissipate the full force of your intentions. Work with the particular zones you select in and around your home and office. Take time to set clear intentions and then enhance each of your chosen areas deliberately.

Once you have begun to notice results from these initial efforts, then proceed to activate and strengthen the chi in the next bagua zone that commands your attention. The bagua and your life are mirrors. Watch as the magic is revealed!

Chapter 5

Remedies for Common Problems

In order to improve the feng shui of your home, office, or garden, you need to learn specific remedies, commonly called "cures," that can enhance the harmonious flow of chi in those spaces. These include mirrors, sounds, scents, and crystals. Feng shui solutions are useful to correct or offset the impact of a design flaw, such as an oddly shaped or missing zone of the bagua. The intrinsic power of the remedies, combined with how you resonate with them and with your intentions, contributes to their effectiveness.

Before placing any cures, it is essential to prepare the space where you want to enhance chi. This is a step-by-step process. First, it is important to clear out clutter and then to circulate stagnant chi by space-clearing. These activities create positive energy that supports and amplifies your chosen intentions and desires. There could be huge, negative effects were you to enhance and activate the chi of a messy or dirty area!

Clear your clutter

You don't want to repeat the past, do you? No. You want to create a new life, a new you, and a new future that supports your intentions. But how can you create a powerful now and a fulfilling future when you are inundated with incomplete projects and the paraphernalia of previous years? If the future you are planning holds none of the old patterns, then you need to remove objects from the past that are holding you back. When I go to my office to work or write, I make sure that my desk area is clear of old business, yesterday's mail, and last week's messages. Likewise, it is important to clear away distractions in order to focus and move forward.

Another good reason to unclutter your space is simplicity. Simplifying life by getting rid of unnecessary possessions can bring us greater happiness. True happiness does not lie in accumulating material objects, but in reducing and relinquishing them. You see, unhappiness represents the psychological distance between what we already have and what we want. By accepting our current circumstances, this gap dissolves. So does the sense of unhappiness.

Step 1: Identifying your clutter

Take a good long look around your home, not just a cursory look. Spend time looking inside your cabinets, drawers, and closets. Whew! If you're like most people, I bet you didn't realize what an accumulation of stuff you would find. Now ask yourself some questions. What are you actually using? How often? How regularly?

Do you always reach for the same coffee cup, even when you have another 15 in your cupboard? Do you wear the same clothes repeatedly although your closet is crammed full? Are you planning to purchase new towels and bed linens once you feng shui your home? Then consider how many old towels and linens already fill up your linen closet. Are you also keeping a leaning tower of plastic food containers in your kitchen cupboards, ones that you never use?

Until now you may not have considered the amount of energy, time, and space that are being taken up by all your unneeded extra stuff. As we discussed in the Introduction, the vital energy of the universe infuses all your belongings. The overall chi of your home gets "watered down" and tainted by possessions that you don't love, use, or need, or which remind you of unpleasant memories and difficult people.

Trust your instincts. Assess the energy of anything you are considering getting rid of. How does it feel? When it has any negative connotations you would be better off releasing it. On an energetic level, every item contains the chi from its source and everyone that has come in contact with it. You should ask: Where did it come from originally? Who made it? Who owned it before you? Anything associated with unhappy or uncomfortable memories can subtly drain your chi. Let it go.

After you have gone through the house evaluating your belongings, then check your attic, basement, and garage. Figure out how much clutter resides in these spaces. People like me, who don't have garages, learn to live with fewer belongings. You can, too. Since a divorce years ago and the necessary "downsizing" that accompanied the stressful event, I have slowly become good at eliminating most of my clutter. I no longer keep unnecessary or unloved belongings.

Do you recall that in the Introduction we talked about the fact that your home, your environment, and your possessions are an energetic representation of you? Well, who is the person you want to be? Do the objects in your home reflect that image or another?

Because you are probably beginning to get a clear picture of how much stuff you have accumulated, let's move to the next step.

Step 2: Reducing your clutter

It is worthwhile to set aside a specific date and time to begin uncluttering. You may want to start on a weekend. Or if a whole weekend seems too much, set aside a single Saturday or Sunday. Write down your start date in your calendar in bold letters. Make it a firm commitment.

My clients have found that the process of eliminating their clutter usually starts out as drudgery. They have the sense that it is going to be an overwhelming task. But then it begins to feel energizing! And more importantly, it gets easier and easier. Because clearing clutter is a form of emotional and physical release, there should be a new sense of lightness and freedom at the end of it. When you are finished, you won't believe how good you feel. It is like going to a spa for week.

Please be sure to incorporate breaks into your plan. Uncluttering could be a major chore, and you need to pace yourself. Schedule time out for a walk on the beach or in the park. You should give yourself permission to stop and have a cup of tea or coffee and relax every so often.

Once you have identified where to begin, you need to gather supplies. What you need is predicated by whether you're in the garage, basement, attic, and so on. Some spaces are more "cluttery" by nature than others. You definitely need plenty of bags. Use strong 30-gallon garden or trash bags. Also keep four or more large boxes handy. With a marking pen, label each box. Start filling them up with your stuff. My sons came up with the following categories for belongings, which I have adopted:

Keepers: "I'm keeping these items." These are things you want to keep, but that can go into a storage box for the time being. It can be beneficial to rearrange or rotate the objects and accessories that you use and display in your environment, such as vases, photos, treasures, and mementos. Changing the objects in your home from time to time influences the movement of chi. No matter how many or how few collectibles you insist on keeping, it is important to create an organized storage space for them.

Tossers: "I'm throwing these items away." Be aggressive! These are things that can immediately go into the trash or be recycled. This box works especially well when you are discarding old files, paperwork, and mail, old magazines and newspapers, and dead plants. Include items in this category that are broken, cracked, and need repairs. If you haven't fixed it yet, why wait? You would probably have fixed it were the item truly necessary for your life.

Givers: "I'm donating these items." These are the things you want to give away. Some can go to friends, members of your family, or coworkers. There are also many thrift stores, charities, and local libraries that accept all kinds of household objects and books, as long as they are in decent shape. You can get tax deductions for donations. Remember the yard-sale adage: One man's trash is another man's treasure. If you are so inclined, consider throwing a yard sale. Be sure to schedule a thrift store to pick up what doesn't sell. Don't bring any of those leftovers back into the house!

Thinkers: "I'm not sure what I want to do with these items." Give yourself 10 days to decide about objects that didn't naturally fall into one of the other three categories. But be sure to put them in the box. Perhaps the item is a memento from a past relationship, a special keepsake you stored for your grown-up children from their infancy or early childhood, or a family heirloom left in your care to pass on that you have no desire to use yourself. These could also be items that make you say, "I *might* need that some day." At the end of 10 days make your decision. Is it a keeper, a tosser, or a giver?

The job of eliminating clutter is to become conscious of all the elements in your home, especially how they affect you at the heart and soul level, and then to bring those elements into alignment with your purpose and the possibilities of the future.

As you begin to move through each room clearing your clutter and the remnants of your past, ask yourself the following questions about every item:

1. Do I love this?
2. Do I use this?
3. Do I want or need this?

Take a last look around the room when you are finished putting items in boxes. What's left? Did you go through the kids' old video games? Did you review your CD and video collections? Your books? Are there accessories that have outlived their usefulness? Do you have old table linens from your single days? Or bed sheets purchased to enhance a former relationship? Are you keeping unwanted gifts? Were curtains left hanging by the previous homeowner? Do you have faded pillows on the couch? Make a decision.

 ## Rob's story

Rob was a 35-year-old man who hired me to consult with him on ways to simplify his home and remove clutter. As we were going through the uncluttering process, we stopped in the living room in front of a handsome quilt that his deceased grandmother had made, which lay draped over the arm of his couch. He admitted he did not have fond feelings for his grandmother because she had been abusive and mean to him. Nonetheless he felt compelled to keep the quilt because it was a family heirloom of sorts.

I gently explained to Rob that he had other alternatives. He could give the quilt away to another member of his family who perhaps hadn't had the same experience of his grandmother, or he could wrap it up carefully for safekeeping and put it away in the attic or basement. He was delighted! No one had ever given him "permission" before to remove it. After the quilt was gone, a tangible uplifting feeling drifted into the room. Without the frequent reminder of emotional pain inflicted upon him by his grandmother's energetic presence, he was able to begin the healing process of forgiveness.

Step 3: Spring cleaning

Now that you have eliminated the excess clutter, give your space a good "spring cleaning." Yep. Sorry to have to tell you, but the next step to good feng shui is serious housework! Clean the windows, dust the furniture, wash and vacuum the floors, and sweep out the cobwebs and dust bunnies. Make this an important priority. There is no point in spending time and effort on feng shui if your space is dirty.

Take the time and don't allow any interruptions. Housekeeping can be a form of mindfulness and meditation, a spiritual practice that puts you in the moment, if you approach it in this fashion. Use natural and non-toxic cleaning products as much as possible. Open the windows and let the fresh air in.

Basic housekeeping is an integral part of good feng shui. On one level, you are washing away dirt and clearing debris. On another, energetic level, you are also clearing away negative chi. You may be amazed at the increased clarity of mind and perception that can result from cleaning your home. There could be an atmospheric shift in the life force of the space. Any heightened awareness, intuition, and shift to more positive energy absolutely does affect you and resonate through everything that you do in your life.

When you have eliminated clutter and finished cleaning your space, you will have taken a big leap towards creating an environment that you want to escape to, not from. It is time for the next step.

Space-clearing rituals

Space-clearing rituals are used to cleanse the energy of an environment. In ancient cultures, where the intangible realm is better understood than in the modern Western world, rituals for space-clearing are commonplace. It is only recently that we, too, have begun embracing these powerful rituals. The world of energy can be mysterious and subtle. Yet, magical and strange as it may seem, space-clearing works. As a Realtor and feng shui practitioner, I always ask my clients if they would like to have a space-clearing and blessing ritual done for their new home before they move in. You may also want to consider space-clearing when you are making changes in your life or experiencing a challenging situation.

Most of us have had the experience of walking into a home where the occupants frequently argue and being able to sense the heavy, uncomfortable atmosphere. We have also sensed the lively energy infusing a room when a celebration is in process. If you were buying a new home, you wouldn't dream of moving into it without it being thoroughly cleaned. Imagine the unseen layers of energy that have accumulated during the lives of the previous owners. Life situations can bring on a spectrum of feelings, ranging from anger to depression to fear. Happy and positive experiences of previous occupants should not worry you. Rather you should be concerned about illnesses, death, or resentments that could have built up in your space like layers of unseen grime.

Before you start any clearing ritual it is important to cleanse yourself. Take a shower or a bath, wash your hair, and brush your teeth. Put on clean clothes and remove jewelry, belts, and watches. Particularly avoid space-clearing when you do not feel well or are unhappy or angry. Also do not perform any of these rituals with another person who may be unhappy, unstable, or depressed.

Here are some basic methods of space-clearing:

Salt: When cleaning out attics, basements, garages, storage areas, and closets, place bowls of salt water in the corners of the space. Use a ratio of one cup of salt for every eight cups of water. Add a tablespoon of baking soda. Put the salt water in plastic bowls that you can throw away. Leave these in the space for 10 days, replenishing the salt water every three days.

Clapping: Clapping is a very simple means of space-clearing. Be sure to wash your hands before this ritual. You are going to go clockwise beginning at your front door. Move steadily around your space, clapping in every nook and corner. Start low, next to the floor, and clap swiftly, moving upward towards the ceiling. Reach as far up as you can. A ladder is useful when a room has high, vaulted ceilings. When you start, you may notice that your clapping sounds muted. Then, as you clear the stuck energy in the room, your clapping becomes crisper and clearer. Keep your purpose in mind and the results could amaze you.

When you are finished clapping around the perimeter of the space, be sure to wash your hands thoroughly again. This helps remove negative energy that may have stuck to your body during the ritual.

Bells: Find a bell with a beautiful, clear tone, one whose sound you enjoy. You will instinctively know when you have the right bell by listening carefully. Is it pure and clear? Use the bell in a similar manner to the clapping ritual. Move clockwise around the perimeter of your space, going upwards from floor to ceiling and spending extra time in the corners. Corners are where energy often becomes stuck. As you ring the bell, be sure to create a continuous tone. Chime it again each time the previous tone begins to diminish.

Smudging: Smoke from burning herbs has been used throughout the ages by many cultures around the world as part of their religious ceremonies. The smoke is used to purify the energy of the ritual space and of the ritual participants. Although many herbs can be used for smudging, the most common ones are sage, cedar, and sweet grass.

Sage has special purification powers. It is burned to drive out negative feelings or influences, thus protecting the home. Cedar is burned for the purpose of cleansing while praying. The prayers rise on the cedar smoke to the Creator. Cedar is especially effective in dispelling negative energy. Sweet grass is one of the most sacred plants to the Plains Indians. It is frequently burned after either sage or cedar to bring in positive energies. The fresh, clean smell of sweet grass drives away negative thoughts and bad spirits.

Resins are also used frequently, such as copal, myrrh, and frankincense. They can be burned on a charcoal wafer or added to burning herbs. Copal is a resin from the copal tree that grows in Mexico and Central America. It is burned for purification and protection. Myrrh is burned to bring peace to a situation, to understand personal sorrow, and to expand spiritual awareness. Frankincense is burned for protection as well as purification. It also fosters the focus of attention.

Smudge sticks, which are bundles of purifying herbs, may be purchased in most alternative bookstores, natural food markets, and New Age shops. You can also make your own smudge sticks using local, indigenous ingredients.

You will need the following for your smudging ritual:

- A smudge stick.
- A shell or bowl.
- A feather (optional).

To create smudge smoke, first light your bundle of herbs. After the herbs have ignited, blow out the fire. The bundle should continue to smolder and smoke. When you are holding or carrying smudge sticks, use a fireproof container to catch any sparks. I prefer using something from the natural world, such as an abalone shell or a favorite piece of earthen pottery. Some people use metal bowls. You may need to put a hot pad underneath. Be creative and follow your own instincts.

Before performing a smudging ceremony, smudge yourself to cleanse the energy of your personal energy field. In her book *Sacred Space,* Denise Linn suggests the following practice. Cup your hands and bring the smoke towards your body. Start by wafting the smoke over your closed eyes and say, "That my eyes may see clearly." Repeat the movement around your head and say, "That my thoughts may be clear." Lastly, bring the smoke to your chest and say, "That my heart may be pure and open." If you are smudging with a partner, repeat the process with him or her. This ritual will provide balance and grounding before you begin smudging your space.

To smudge a room, or your entire home, place the smoking herbs in your shell or bowl, holding it in your non-dominant hand. A right-handed person would use her left hand. As you engage in the ritual, it is particularly powerful to smudge with the use of a feather. Feathers are a powerful connection to the world of animal spirits and totems. Hold the feather in your dominant hand and begin waving and moving the smoke lightly around the room.

Begin in the easternmost corner of the room and smudge the room in a clockwise direction spending extra time in the corners. You may invoke or pray for certain wishes or intentions as you smudge. Always remember to stay focused and aware.

When you have completed smudging the circumference of the room, stand in the center and ask Spirit to purify and cleanse the room. At this time, you can say a simple smudging prayer, such as: "Spirit of our home, bring the energies of Healing, Love, Abundance, and Peace to this room, this house, and this family. For this and for all our blessings, we give thanks." Better yet, make up your own prayer. This allows your own heart and soul to speak.

To complete your space-clearing, light candles, burn incense, sprinkle the areas with holy water, and/or set out fresh flowers and fruit. Space-clearing is enhanced when completed with the ringing of a bell. Offer prayers to the angels, saints, or spirit guardians of the house and say any affirmations or intentions that are important to you.

A word of caution: When you have finished your smudging ceremony, be certain the burning herbs are completely extinguished. They can sometimes appear to be out, yet continue to smolder.

Now your space is prepared and you are ready to begin placing cures.

Common feng shui problems

Poison arrows

This is the term used to describe sharp angles and straight lines that point towards you in any environment. The idea is that the energy produced by poison arrows is negative and "cutting" because it is knifelike when it emanates from a 90-degree angle. You especially don't want a poison arrow over or aiming at your bed, where it could "cut" into your relationship and your health!

Poison arrows can be caused by:

- Square or angular columns.
- Ceiling beams.
- Ceiling fans.
- Corners. Corners may be from exterior or interior walls or those found on furniture, such as desks, tables, and cabinets.

When you cannot avoid a built-in poison arrow, you can cure it with a remedy that reflects the energy, such as a mirror or a crystal. Square columns can be remedied by putting a cure in front of them

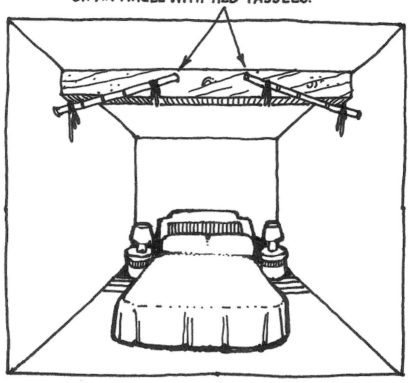

Figure 5.1. How to cure a ceiling beam.

such as a plant. If you have a beam overhead and cannot move your
bed, couch, or desk from under it, hang two bamboo flutes with red
tassels from it on an angle. This lifts cutting energy upwards. (See
Figure 5.1.)

Front doors

There are several common problems often related to the front
entrance. These include disrepair, overgrowth, and dead plants. As
this is considered the overall "mouth of chi" to your home, it is essential that it be attractive and easy to approach. Good fortune and prosperity need to be able to find you and come in!

Keep your gates and fences in working condition. Make your front
door look pleasant. Apply a fresh coat of paint, use nice hardware,
polish the hinges, and clean off the cobwebs. Trim your hedges and
overgrowth and prune plants away from the entrance. Remove dried
or dead plants from around your front doorstep.

Dark areas

Chi can flow smoothly, flow too fast, or be stagnant. Dark areas
hold stagnant energy, which is negative and underactivated. How could
you manifest anything without enough energy? The most relevant cure
for darkness is bright lighting, which moves chi and uplifts the tone of
any space.

Doorways and hallways

In homes where the front door is directly in a path with the back
door or a large picture window, and where the space between contains no furnishings or fixtures to break the flow of energy, the chi
comes in swiftly and goes out just as swiftly. To prevent the vital life
force from escaping, hang a wind chime in the space between the
doors (see Figure 5.2). Placing crystals, hanging chandeliers, or installing a decorative screen can also cure the problem. Use similar
cures in long hallways, where chi also moves too rapidly.

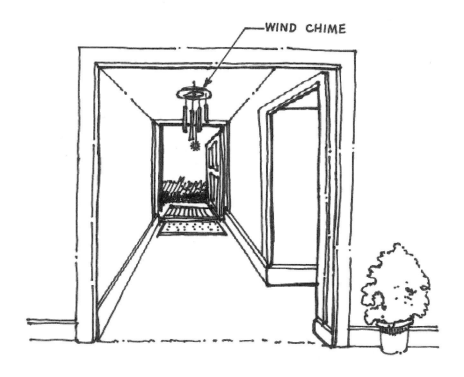

Figure 5.2. How to remedy vital energy from escaping through a long hallway and door.

Beds

The position of your bed is one of the most important placements in feng shui. You spend a lot of time in bed, and when you are sleeping or resting you are vulnerable. How chi crosses your bed impacts you tremendously. The bed is significant to general health and well-being, not to mention your marriage or intimate relationship.

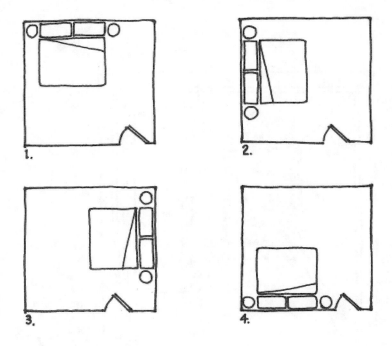

Figure 5.3. Bed placements. Positions 1 and 2 are good feng shui placements; avoid bed placements in positions 3 and 4.

A general guideline is that anyone lying in bed should have a view of the entire room and the door, but not be in a direct path with the door. This is because the door is the "mouth of chi" to the bedroom. When chi enters, it exerts a powerful force over anything and anyone in line with it. The placement of the bed in positions 1 and 2 in Figure 5.3 are appropriate. Avoid placing the bed in the positions 3 and 4.

Bathrooms

Bathrooms are tricky and can host a number of potential feng shui problems. Water runs down drains and energy goes out with it. The cures include putting a mirror on the ceiling above the drain and keeping the bathroom door closed at all times so it is not pulling energy from your whole house.

Toilets are even bigger energy drainers. So routinely keep the toilet lid down. Do not place your bed against the opposite side of the wall where the toilet is located; otherwise it could drain you of energy while you sleep. And be sure the toilet is not in a direct line of sight through the bathroom door.

Leaks

As are drains and toilets, leaks are a common problem for homeowners. Leaky faucets, pipes, hose bibs, and sprinklers pull energy away with the dripping water. Remember that water is symbolic of money. Your wealth can be dripping away if you allow leaks to remain unchecked. Repair all the systems on your property that have leaking or dripping water.

Missing zones

As we discussed in Chapter 4, once you align your bagua over your home, your office, or an individual room, you could discover that a whole zone is missing altogether or indented. This would be because your floor plan is not square or rectangular. The missing area is called "negative space" because it implies a deficit of a form of energy that you need to lead a rich and balanced life. Most homes do have some negative space, although the energy field still *is* there, albeit intangibly. Incorporating cures such as mirrors, crystals, and lighting allows you to balance any underrepresented qualities with beneficial, positive chi.

Let us consider the significance of some odd-shaped floor plans. Here are some potential problems and benefits that can arise within each zone:

Journey and Career

- ◆ When this zone is missing or indented, you may frequently become ill.
- ◆ When this zone is projected, you may accrue wealth and typically would have a firm sense of your life's direction.

Self-Wisdom and Knowledge

- ◆ When this zone is missing or indented, you may lack interest in your inner self or self-growth. That lack of interest could apply to life in general or to academic study.

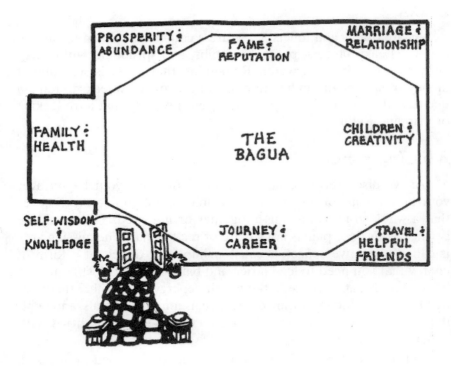

Figure 5.4. Projection of the Health and Family zone.

- When this zone is projected, you may be a good student and typically would be interested in personal development. You probably follow your intuition and meditate.

Family and Health

- When this zone is missing or indented, you may feel a loss of vitality and become sick. You could also experience frequent rifts and estrangements among your extended family and groups of friends.
- When this zone is projected, your family relationships and health are probably strong.

Prosperity and Abundance

- When this zone is missing or indented, you may experience more than your fair share of misfortune in your business and financial affairs.
- When this zone is projected, you are more likely to experience good luck, business success, and abundant blessings of all kinds.

Fame and Reputation

- When this zone is missing or indented, you may be overly concerned with what other people think of you, even suffering from paranoia, and have shaky self-esteem.
- When this zone is projected, the heightened chi it brings is likely to contribute towards attaining great fame and self-realization or achieving illumination.

Marriage and Relationship

- When this zone is missing or indented, you may find it difficult to form long-term romantic relationships and partnerships.
- When this zone is projected, you are more likely to sustain long and happy relationships and partnerships. A note of caution, however: There may also be a tendency to have too many romantic partners.

Children and Creativity

* When this zone is missing or indented, there probably are no children in the home or, if there are, their creative and artistic juices are not being fully encouraged or inspired. You may also feel stifled creatively.
* When this zone is projected, it is likely that you and your family are artistic, creative, and social. There may be many children (and friends) running in and out.

Helpful Friends and Travel

* When this zone is missing or indented, you may have problems with your coworkers, bankers, or advisers.
* When this area is projected, you probably are philanthropically minded, contributing your time and money to the less fortunate, and could travel a great deal both for business and for pleasure.

Feng shui cures

There are 10 categories of basic remedies that can be used to balance and activate the chi in any area. A rule of thumb: Always be sure to match the size to the situation. A large room, or an area that contains extremely stagnant or fast-moving chi, would require more extensive remedies. When selecting a cure, choose one that suits your decorative style and personal taste. A remedy is going to be most effective if it is something with which you truly resonate. Whether it's a color or a special object, you must enjoy it and even cherish it for it to be beneficial.

Light and bright objects

Light and bright objects include mirrors, natural and refractive lights, candles, and cut glass. Use cut glass that is clear and round or faceted to adjust the direction of the flow of energy through a window, a hallway, or another area where it moves too fast or dissipates, such as when the ceilings are very high. Cut glass can also disperse negative chi. Use lighting to brighten a dark area, bringing positive chi in. Keep your windows clean to allow in sunlight. Hang a crystal

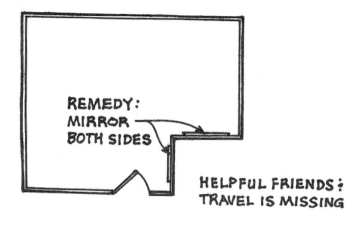

Figure 5.5. Mirrors as a cure for a missing bagua zone.

chandelier in the dining room to heighten the chi being drawn into the space.

Mirrors are a common feng shui cure and it is important to understand how to use them properly. Mirrors can redirect beneficial energy into a space and they can send away energy that is problematic. Therefore they are an especially good cure for a missing area of the bagua. By hanging a mirror on the wall opposing a missing area you can direct energy into that void. You can also hang a mirror within the missing or indented zone to create the illusion of space, thereby strengthening the chi that is already present, however minimally. (See Figure 5.5.) In stagnant areas, such as a doorway where a wall is located immediately within the entrance, mirrors can also enhance the circulation of chi.

Be sure your mirrors are spotlessly clean and do not have decorative or fine lines or veins. Avoid smoky or tiled mirrors made of many sections. Also be sure they are of good quality. Broken, damaged, faded, or scratched mirrors could produce a strong, undesirable effect. Oval or round mirrors are better than square or rectangular ones. In

addition, when hanging a mirror, the height is important. Make sure
that anyone who looks in the mirror can see the upper portion of his
or her head.

Sound

Sound lifts energy. Music, wind chimes, and Tibetan singing bowls
are wonderful sound cures, especially when you love the tone. Because sound vibrates through your body, it can strengthen your personal energy field.

Music is sacred. It raises the vibration of your space. Particularly
during meditation or quiet time, music has the ability to enhance,
guide, restore, and heal. Bells are often used to begin and close sacred ceremonies. When bells are rung, their vibration can smooth
the passage of chi and redirect patterns of energy. Tibetan singing
bowls have a unique sacred tone that resonates with the energies of
the spirit world.

Wind chimes can activate yang energy and alleviate negative chi.
They can be used to raise energy trapped beneath low ceilings and to
stop positive energy from going out doorways. Hang your chimes from
the ceiling above your doorway so that when the door is opened it
gently moves them, creating a soft acknowledgment. Be sure the doorbell of your home has a pleasing sound, too.

For the purpose of feng shui, wind chimes should be made with
hollow rods. The hollows allow chi to rise. They may be made out of
metal, bamboo, glass, or crystal. It is best to choose a chime whose
tinkling or tone you particularly enjoy. Metal wind chimes are especially good for enhancing the zone of Journey and Career, which is
associated with this element. Bamboo, or other wooden chimes, boosts
the Family and Health zone, which is associated with the wood element.

Wind chimes worked like a charm for a young architect named
Garrison. He had started his own firm three years earlier after leaving
a successful 10-person practice. Economic indicators within his industry were positive and his prospects were promising, yet profits
were not as large as expected. His parents had pitched in financially
to get him through the transition, but business was only okay, not
good. He was eager to repay their investment. In addition, now he was
engaged to be married and wanted to be more financially solid before
the wedding.

Although he was a little skeptical, Jenny, Garrison's fiancée, arranged a feng shui consultation with me. His offices were located in a charming cottage on the fringes of the business district. The building itself was well suited for his type of company. In my opinion, all he needed was to activate the chi a little bit. Garrison was not keen on hanging crystals and Chinese bamboo flutes around his office, but he was willing to consider other options. We agreed on putting wind chimes on the porch near the front door. He was pleasantly surprised to discover that a feng shui cure could match the décor of his offices, and he said he would enjoy the pleasant tinkling of the chimes in the breeze.

Two weeks later, I received an excited telephone call. Garrison and Jenny were delirious with joy. He had landed a huge architectural contract less than 10 days after placing the wind chimes. Call it magick, call it luck, or call it beneficial chi. Garrison, Jenny, and his parents were blissed out!

Nature

Living things bring chi to life. These include plants, flowers, and trees, animals, birds, and fish. The shapes and colors of healthy plants and flowers enhance the positive chi of a space. Avoid using dead or dried plants, flowers, or animal parts. Otherwise, unless a dried flower or dried flower arrangement has special sentimental value, use only quality fabric or silk flowers and plants that are clean and well cared for. If the ones you have are dirty, dusty, old, and brittle, you need to replace them. Plants with large and/or rounded or oval leaves are especially good for keeping chi circulating. So avoid plants with sharp, thorny, or long spiky leaves. Those would cut chi.

Fish symbolize prosperity and wealth. But be sure to keep their aquariums and bowls clean and fresh. Outdoor ponds of fish should be kept from getting stagnant and dirty. Bird cages and cat boxes must be kept clean and tidy as well. How you care for the living creatures that share your home influences the nature of the chi within it.

Heavy objects

Rocks and other large objects, such as statues and other sculpture, create a solid and stabilizing effect on the chi in your environment. Heavy objects ground and anchor the chi. Sculpture is a good cure because as a piece of artwork it is endowed with meaning. Boulders are infused with the power and beauty of nature.

Choose sculpture according to your personal taste. A large Buddha or sculpture of a *mudra* (a Hindu meditative hand posture) can be a powerful enhancement to any area of the bagua, but most especially to the zone of Self-Wisdom and Knowledge. It can be a powerful statement of your intention to grow spiritually and psychologically. Likewise, a sensuous sculpture of a couple in loving embrace placed in the Marriage and Relationship zone can support a loving relationship and marriage. A large stone water fountain placed in the Prosperity and Abundance corner of your garden can enhance your wealth.

Color

Colors have general associations and meaning in feng shui. Each zone of the bagua is associated with a specific color. Therefore you can add more of the associated color to enhance the flow of chi in that specific area. And, as we read in Chapter 3, color can balance the interaction of the five elements in a room. The most important aspect of color, however, is whether it pleases you. Regardless of what zone or element that the color is attributed to, how does it make you feel?

Colors have different associations depending on the culture you live in. Note the expressions "feeling sad and blue" or "being green with envy." In the Western world, yellow is also associated with cowardice (jaundice) as well as remembrance (tie a yellow ribbon). Red is sometimes associated with anger ("seeing red"). However, in feng shui, red stands for fame, reputation, passion, and strength.

Color has been used as a therapeutic medium since ancient times. Today color therapists believe that the body and mind react with colors, affecting everything from how we act to how we feel and creating a significant impact on our spirits. In practical application, color includes all the shades and tones of its full spectrum. For example, red includes orange and pink. Yellow includes cream, taupe, and brown. Black includes charcoal, gray, and midnight blue.

The essence of colors

- **Red:** Red uplifts, stimulates, and brightens your energy level. In whichever room you use red, be aware of its tremendous energy. This is the color of romance, power, activity, excitement, and fame.
- **Pink:** Pink softens the energy of a room. This is the color associated with relationships and romance.
- **Purple:** Purple attracts energy and enhances spirituality. This is the color of wealth and fame. Use purple as an accent color, rather than the main color scheme for an entire room.
- **Orange:** Orange enhances creativity. This color is warm, romantic, happy, social, flamboyant, and confident. Orange is good for a dining room or a family room.
- **Yellow:** Yellow lifts and brightens your mood and energy. It stimulates the intellect and creativity. It affects concentration and academic achievement. Yellow is most appropriate for a home office or a child's bedroom.
- **Green:** Green is a gentle energy, cooling and soothing. It enhances balance and harmony. This is the color of healing, stability, nature, family, and wealth.
- **Blue:** Blue is the color associated with self-knowledge and spiritual devotion. It evokes feelings of peace and tranquility. It is a good color for a meditation room or the bedroom of a hyperactive child.
- **Brown:** Brown relaxes and slows down one's energy level. It is the color of the earth. Avoid too much brown, as it can dull the spirit.
- **Black:** Black is a very powerful non-color. It evokes power, success, career, knowledge, and mystery. Black focuses on the inner world. Use black to accessorize and highlight. Too much black in one room can be depressing and overwhelming.
- **White:** White enhances spiritual attunement. It is associated with purity, cleanliness, and refinement. It is the color of every color combined. Just be careful of an all-white room, which could feel sterile and uncomfortable. People with white bedrooms tend to give themselves away without receiving enough nurturing in return.

Moving objects

Moving objects are associated with wind, which is a source of chi. Therefore mobiles, windsocks, banners and flags, windmills, whirligigs, tassels, and weathervanes all stimulate and activate energy where they are placed. Mobiles may be placed inside your home as a substitute for a wind chime, if you would prefer something quieter. But, in general, moving objects are best placed in the garden or outdoors.

It has been said that elemental beings, such as Fairies, Elves, Gnomes, and water Sprites, are attracted to gardens with colorful and moving objects, such as windsocks, banners, and whirligigs. Their presence is considered extremely positive. Consider installing a flagpole on your property to lift energy in places where the land is lower than the road or to strengthen the energy of a missing bagua.

Energy objects

Energy objects are those items with sacred meaning to you. These can include religious relics, objects, and talismans, such as figurines of angels, saints, and spiritual masters. Icons of Jesus, Mary, Buddha, Kuan Yin, and other favorite deities represent their divine energy and love. They can bring wisdom, comfort, and guidance to your sacred space. Mystic symbols also add energy and meaning to your space. Experiment with a cross, a Star of David, a menorah, a goblet, a pyramid, rosaries, prayer beads, or runes. Placing these on an altar is one way to enhance your relationship with the qualities they represent. Whatever is inspirational qualifies, even books.

In China, bamboo flutes are regarded as energy objects. Red tassels are added to a bamboo flute so that it resembles an ancient Chinese sword and then it is hung from an overhead beam. They are an effective measure because bamboo grows upward section by section. This upward growth pattern breaks the negative cutting chi that comes from the beam. It symbolically "slices" through the negative, cutting chi.

Water features

Fountains, pools, ponds, aquariums, and water sculptures are a double whammy feng shui cure. Not only do they stimulate the flow of chi, but they are also symbolic of money, wealth, and opportunity. They can be especially powerful cures in the zone of Prosperity and Abundance and in the zone of Journey and Career, where water features can activate networking and an increased flow of clients.

Next time you are in a Chinese restaurant, notice if there isn't an aquarium located near the front door or the cash register. A bowl of gold fish and vases of flowers also activate and enhance water energy.

For maximum financial security, allow water to collect in a generous pond or basin.

Elemental beings are said to be attracted to water features in a garden, as well as to moving objects. They enjoy the sight and sound of sparkling and splashing water. Swimming pools are another excellent feng shui enhancement. Be sure that they are kept clean. If it is possible, install a fountain in the pool to boost its positive influence.

Crystals and gemstones

Crystals and precious and semiprecious gemstones are known for their extraordinary ability to amplify energy levels. They have fascinated people since ancient times. Different stones and crystals resonate with the different energy centers of the body, known as *chakras*, and with different qualities, such as wisdom, clarity, prosperity, and comfort. Many people use them as healing devices and tools of power and wisdom.

Natural crystals, such as clear, smoky, or rose quartz, citrine, and amethyst, are superb cures. They can be polished or raw depending on your preference and what speaks to you energetically. Place crystal balls on tabletops to activate harmonious chi. Hang a crystal on a piece of fishing line or nine-inch long colored ribbon in your window. It is effective even behind your window treatments. The ribbon should be the color of the quality you wish to enhance (see "The Essence of Colors," page 97).

Totems

The belief in house guardians in the form of totems can be found throughout the world. Like the Chinese, Native Americans give credence to the protective spirit of an animal ally or guide, as do Celtic Shamans. Totems can be an important element in making your home a safe and spiritual haven. Each animal possesses unique qualities, and you can draw upon these strengths. The wolf's powers of pathfinding and hunting are legendary. This totem therefore symbolizes finding our path in the world with clarity and keen vision. Rabbit totems are used for invoking fertility.

Your power animal may be your favorite animal since childhood or it may be the type of animal you are irresistibly drawn to as an adult. You may recognize your totem because you tend to share or because you desire to acquire its abilities and characteristics. Animal allies are very individual and the best totem is the one for which you feel the most affinity. It is not unusual for totems to change when you transition from one stage of life to another. Use your own judgment and intuition.

Once you have determined your totem, take time to place physical representations of it, such as statues, carvings, and photographs, around your home. You can either use one totem throughout your entire space or "call forth" several totems that are specific to individual rooms. The bear is often a good choice for the bedroom. They are a dreamer's totem and have healing energy. Elk are considered to be very powerful office totems where you want to evoke feelings of power and stamina. A crow is also a good office totem due to its persistence, cunning, and curiosity.

Installing remedies

When you are ready to place or activate a cure in any zone of the bagua, focus on the particular aspect of your life that it governs. Be still and set a clear intention. Then, in your mind's eye, creatively visualize the intended results or transformation you are seeking, saying an affirmation or prayer that correlates with it. Try the following affirmations or make up your own:

For Journey and Career:

- My career brings me joy and abundance.
- My purpose in life is fulfilling and productive.
- My life's journey flows effortlessly and easily.

For Self-Wisdom and Knowledge:

- Today my noisy thoughts take flight, so that the song of silence may whisper guidance to my heart and soul.
- I safely look within myself and what I see is a wise, kind, and loving me.
- I trust my inner wisdom. I listen to my intuition. It is always there to guide me.

For Family and Health:

- My heart, soul, and mind are powerful healing tools.
- This imbalance holds a healing lesson for me to learn.
- I bless my family with love and acceptance.

For Prosperity and Abundance:

- Today, my prosperity is ever increasing.
- Every day, my life abundantly supports me.
- I am grateful and rejoice in my financial success.

For Fame and Reputation:

- I attract whatever I need for a glorious future.
- I am known for my compassion, wisdom, and integrity.
- I am a unique person, yet one with all of life.

For Marriage and Relationship:

- I am loving and I experience authentic love in my marriage.
- My relationships are loving, compassionate, and joyful.
- I effortlessly create harmonious partnerships.

For Children and Creativity:

- Today I acknowledge the creator within me and I embrace my own unique talents and creative gifts.
- I acknowledge my inner child and I embrace his/her childlike wonder and imagination.
- Today I send heartfelt and unconditional love to all the children in the world.

For Helpful Friends and Travel:

- I am always at the right place to meet the right people at the right time.
- Synchronicity is flowing to me and through me effortlessly.
- I have many wonderful friends and benefactors.

The story of Valerie and Nathan

Valerie and Nathan had been married for three years and were eager to begin a family. But after a few months of simply allowing nature to take its course, Valerie wasn't pregnant. She was doing all the right things: regular exercise, healthy eating habits, and meditation to lower her stress. Nathan was healthy, too. Thus the couple was a bit perplexed. They wanted to move the process along. When they had bought their house two years earlier they purchased a book on feng shui. Now they pulled it out again, looking for help in making babies. From this resource they correctly gathered that they needed to enhance the energy in the bagua zone of Children and Creativity.

The couple located the overall Children and Creativity zone of their home in the dining room. It seemed like a good place to begin. Without further ado, they purchased a large crystal chandelier and hung it over the dining room table, and then scampered off to the bedroom to make those babies. Another six months passed by. Valerie was frequently in tears. She and Nathan went to the doctor to see if there was any physiological reason why she still wasn't getting pregnant. No. "Relax," their doctor said. "You're putting too much pressure on yourselves."

Valerie shared her frustration with a close friend, who asked her if the couple had tried a feng shui remedy. Skeptical at this point, believing that the new chandelier hadn't done them any good, Valerie replied that they had tried feng shui, but that it was a failure. Still when her friend persisted, asking where they got their advice, Valerie confided that they had quickly extrapolated their cure from a book but hadn't tried more than one measure. She was encouraged by her friend to phone me.

I went to see them. Valerie and Nathan had a lovely home, and fortunately it was rectangular, with no missing zones. In my opinion, this gave them a head start! They were sweet and a little bit shy about sharing something so private and personal with a stranger. It was clear they wanted a baby very deeply. Because I have two sons whom I adore, I felt a wave of compassion sweep over me. These young people were so sincere and earnest.

They took me directly to their dining room and, of course, immediately pointed out their crystal chandelier. It was sparkling and attractive and definitely enhanced the chi in the room. I noticed a few other things they had missed however. The table that the chandelier hung above had a glass top and an iron base. Although it was beautiful, it was rectangular and had sharp edges. This would be dangerous for a young toddler to fall or bump into. Two prominent features of the room were a large window on one wall and a large-mouthed fireplace. The window looked out over a canyon, dropping away from the house. Although the view was spacious, the scene would not be a safe place for young children to play. Nothing had been placed within or in front of the fireplace to stop the chi in the room from running right up it and out.

Lastly, the room had an overabundance of the metal element. Their dining room decor included gold walls, gold carpeting, and gold upholstery on the chairs. This was a wrong choice for the intention Valerie and Nathan had in mind. You see, the element associated with babies, young children, and new growth is wood. Not only was there no wood in this room, but the overabundance of metal element would have cut through any wood had it been present.

The first order of business I suggested was to eliminate some of the metal, introduce wood, and be sure the rest of the five elements were in balance. To accomplish this, they replaced the dining room table with a round wood table and had their chairs reupholstered in a soft green color. They replaced the carpeting with another matching soft green and painted the walls off-white.

Next, we balanced the wood element throughout their house and we also introduced cures to the zones of Children and Creativity within every room, using resonant symbols. We placed Nathan's old collection of toy trains in the family room. Valerie placed a small ceramic bowl she had made as a little girl in the kitchen. They hung a quilt that Nathan's grandmother had made when he was a small boy over a chair in the master bedroom. We even reworked the bedroom that would eventually become the nursery. Previously they had been afraid to create a baby room, but little by little, as we placed the new enhancements around their home, they began to feel more and more empowered to move forward with their intentions and their dreams. They decided to go ahead and allow themselves to create a space, both literally and psychologically, for the new child.

Blessedly, 11 weeks later, I got the call! Valerie was pregnant and the prognosis was excellent. She and Nathan were over-the-top ecstatic, so thrilled in fact that they sent me a bottle of champagne with a note saying they were not going to be imbibing for the next nine months. In due time (no pun intended), baby Alexandra came home to her new room and her new life because her mom and dad had stayed the course.

Energy always goes where attention flows. The couple had a profound love and intense desire to have a child. So intent was their focus when they redid their rooms and placed their feng shui cures that they had already grown to know and love their child-waiting-to-be before Valerie was even pregnant. The baby's soul began to reveal itself to them. It was as though they slowly became connected to Alexandra in the cosmic ethers, who was simply waiting for her opportunity to come to live on the physical plane. And this drew her home.

Chapter 6

Evaluating Your Surroundings

Feng shui practitioners respect the natural landscape and are sensitive to the quality of the air, water, flora, and fauna. It is also generally wise to evaluate surrounding roads and neighboring properties for any location. Another primary consideration is whether yin and yang energy in the outer world is well balanced. These are fundamental to the life force in your community and on your street, as well as in the interior of your residence or place of business.

In this chapter, you will learn to assess the feng shui of the general region, as well as the physical structures and essential tone of the energy in the community surrounding your home or office.

Evaluating the natural environment

Years ago, when my husband and I first moved to western Los Angeles from Seattle, my hometown, we began traveling up the coast to Santa Barbara to spend an occasional weekend getaway. We were naturally drawn to the energy of Santa Barbara. I was so compelled to live in this place that it was as though I heard God calling me. Both of us were attracted to the energy and feeling of the overall area and community, but most specifically by Montecito, a small enclave neighboring Santa Barbara.

The natural landscape of the Santa Barbara region has excellent feng shui. People who come to visit often cannot put their finger on why it feels so wonderful. But I know that it is in the balance and scale of the five elements, which are all featured prominently. We are nestled between high mountains and the ocean, with hills protecting us on both sides. We have clean air, water, and abundant sunshine. When a community or region has naturally good feng shui, you can sense it. You may not be able to determine why, but you will be subtly drawn to the area.

Hills

When a home is situated so that the ground slopes down and away from its sides or back, this topography can create a sensation of insecurity and possibly lead to a loss of prosperity. It would be exposed to the wind and water would flow downhill away from it. So do not choose a house perched right on the top of a hill. If your property slopes, be sure that the back of your house is situated higher than the front. Otherwise chi entering your house will flow down to the lower level and drain out.

When there is a higher range of hills or mountains nearby to protect your home, the chi is going to be better. Try to choose a home where the front door is on the opposite side of the house from high hills, however. If your house faces a large hill in front of it, it is likely that you could face financial obstacles and hardships. It is better to have these chi blockers behind you.

Waterways

When analyzing the feng shui of a body of water, notice its physical characteristics. Maybe you live by a narrow creek, a large lake, or a vast sea or ocean. What are its shape and speed of flow? Is it meandering or rapid? What are its width and depth, color and state of cleanliness?

Make sure that waterways around your location are not stagnant, but flowing. Clean, slow-flowing waterways bring positive energy, particularly when they meander in front of the home, rather than behind it. Be sure that you perceive this water feature, whether it is natural or man-made, as flowing towards you or the front door, rather than away. Water exerts a powerful influence on wealth and prosperity. An outward flow could indicate a significant financial loss.

If there are no waterways near or around your home, use your imagination in the placement of ponds, waterfalls, pools, and fountains that would add positive chi.

Flora and fauna

Notice your surrounding vegetation. Is it lush and alive, or are there dead and dying plants on dry rocky ground? Can you sense the energy of the living earth? To cultivate awareness, look for rich vibrant plants and the sound of happily chirping birds. Healthy vegetation that gets plenty of sunlight and water is a sign of positive chi.

A bank of trees behind a house gives occupants a sense of stability and security. Just make sure that trees are not blocking the view of your front door from the street or your garden gate. Although we will touch on this more in Chapter 7, suffice it to say here that trees too close to an entrance can obstruct positive chi. Healthy trees in a neighborhood indicate positive energy.

Observing birds and animals can help you sense the energy of a neighborhood. Listen for the sounds of Nature, water, and birds. Are there any annoying animal sounds, such as barking dogs? Are there stray animals? Do owners clean up after their dogs? Notice if there seem to be too many crows, seagulls, or pigeons, as these scavenging birds spread garbage and disease. What about bugs and insects? Do you want to live where bugs and insects rule?

Figure 6.1. Trees obstructing the entrance to a house.

Look for a healthy, clean neighborhood with chirping birds, butterflies, hummingbirds, and well-cared-for pets. The sounds and sights of Nature are a natural feng shui high. Although man-made sounds such as wind chimes hold good chi, the soothing, natural sounds of Mother Nature are preferable.

The importance of natural sunlight cannot be overstated. Human beings need the natural energy of the sun. Even if your home is not in the "Sunbelt," you can choose to live in a location that allows for as much sunlight as is possible. However, if your home is in an area that gets quite hot, especially in the summer, plant deciduous trees around your house and property to provide needed shade.

Assessing the energy of a neighborhood

As a general rule, the condition of a neighborhood reflects the interior of the residents' homes. People who maintain the condition of their neighborhoods and care about their communities usually also take good care of themselves, their families, and their homes. So start by becoming familiar with the neighborhood in which you are interested in living. Is it well kept? Litter-free? Do unsavory people loiter about? Are residents friendly?

Please keep a few other things in mind when you are choosing where to live:

* What sort of community are you looking for? Are you most interested in schools, parks, recreation, restaurants, or shopping?

* What kind of energy attracts you? Are you naturally drawn to an environment that is uplifting, serene, and comfortable? Are you looking for excitement and cultural institutions?

* Walk around the neighborhood or community. Consider what it feels like. Make note of your sensory impressions. What do you *see*? *Hear*? *Smell*? Images define our experience of a place and how we see ourselves fitting in.

* How do the five elements balance and influence this community? Use the list in the box on page 110 as a guide to determine whether or not your area has harmony. It can be helpful to try to sense the energetic qualities of the elements, not just their obvious associations and characteristics. It might be worthwhile to go back and review the cycles of creation and destruction in Chapter 3, as these tools can help you assess how the five elements are represented in an area.

The 5 elements in your community

- **Wood:** Do you recall that the wood element is associated with trees? Forests, individual trees, shrubs, flowers, plants, and natural or mani-cured landscapes represent different facets of the wood element. So do shapes that resemble trees, such as tall buildings, columns, and pillars. A city with many narrow high-rise buildings denotes a strong wood energy, as would any region that includes lush green forests. Wood is also repre-sented in the "new growth" of a community. So if there is a lot of con-struction going on, your neighborhood probably contains an abundance of wood. The wood element is associated with the color green.

- **Fire:** Universities, art galleries, bookstores, and factories are symbolic of fire energy. Stores that sell electrical items, such as computers and TVs, embody this energy, too. So do triangular buildings shaped like the Eiffel Tower, the Pyramids, or the Empire State Building. Mountainous peaks and hot, sunny locations are both abundant with the fire element. It is also associated with the color red.

- **Earth:** The energy of the earth element relates to the land on which we live. Buildings and dwellings that are square or rectangular are symbolic of earth energy. Materials such as brick, adobe, stucco, and tile also embody earth. Dry, flat desert regions are abundant with natural earth force. The earth element is associated with the colors brown, cream, and yellow.

- **Metal:** Architectural structures that feature domes and arches are asso-ciated with the metal element, as are oval or round-shaped buildings, such as the Roman Coliseum. Building materials and fixtures of iron, steel, chrome, copper, or brass are abundant evidence of metal energy, as are the silver and gold found in churches and elaborately decorated homes. Surfaces of marble, granite, flagstone, and rocks, and landscap-ing that uses boulders, natural rocks, and sculptures made of metal or stone also contain the metal element. In addition, geographic regions full of smooth rolling hills possess the energy of metal.

- **Water:** Areas that have natural bodies of water, such as oceans, lakes, or rivers, embody the water element. Manmade fountains, ponds, pools, and waterfalls also have properties of this energy. So do buildings that have free-flowing shapes, such as the Los Angeles Design Center in West Hollywood (also known as the Blue Whale). Flow is symbolic of the essence of water. Buildings with an abundance of windows and glass likewise are considered watery. The water element is associated with the colors gray, black, and dark blue.

Specific scenarios to avoid

You do not want to reside near certain businesses and institutions where negative energy gathers and congregates. These include:

Cemeteries: These emphasize the energy of death. If you already live near a cemetery, you can suffuse your home and property with the energy of life and the living in several ways. Frequently bless your home using one of the purification or smudging rituals from Chapter 5, sprinkle holy water in the four corners of your property, or place a figurine or statue of a saint, angel, or deity in your garden or on your porch. Visualize an umbrella of white light over your home. Place or plant plenty of living trees and colorful flowers around your home.

Prisons: These emphasize the energy of crime and limitations. If you are near a prison and cannot move, place a hanging crystal, wind chime, or mirror on the exterior wall facing towards the prison building.

Hospitals: These emphasize sickness and accidents. However, if you are in frequent or potential need of medical care, this may be a good area for you. Nonetheless, to mitigate any possible negative chi, place pots of colorful flowers, banners, or windsocks on your front porch.

Police stations: These reinforce the energy of danger and crime. To deflect any potential negative chi from this kind of institution, first be sure that your home is literally and psychologically (to you) burglarproof. Be certain that your windows and doors can lock securely. Live pets, especially dogs, will enhance the chi of safety and provide you with a greater sense of security.

Airports: Avoid buying a home in the flight path of a nearby airport. The exhaust and noise can be debilitating to your health and well-being. If you are in a flight path, keep your home clutter-free and clean. Invest in an air purifier for your home. Regularly do purification rituals to keep any negative chi from becoming stagnant in your home.

Railroad tracks: Trains not only can cause your home to shake, but they also have the potential psychologically to shake the foundation of your finances, health, and relationships. Use cures associated with the earth element that are stabilizing and grounding, such as large boulders and other heavy objects.

Power stations, wireless antenna sites, and electrical transformers: These sites emit strong electromagnetic fields (EMFs) and radiation. Their impact on feng shui can be enormous. Be sure that your bedroom is on the opposite side of the house, and eliminate, as much as possible, your exposure to EMFs inside your home. (See Chapter 9.)

If you find yourself living at or near one of these institutions, sometimes there is nothing you can do to mitigate or cure the situation. It would be better to move to a different location. Take the following case of Melissa.

Melissa brought me to her home for a consultation. Her marriage had recently ended and she wanted to know whether she should keep the house or sell it and move to a new home that she hoped would have better energy. I found that a tall power pole with a transformer and electrical lines going to several adjacent houses stood in the Marriage and Relationship zone of her property. Interestingly, not only were there dead vines covering the pole, but the vegetation at the base of the pole and throughout the entire flowerbed was unhealthy and dead looking. Her marriage had also become a victim of the hazardous radiation emitting from the transformer.

Assessing structures

Most of the principles of feng shui and chi that we have explored thus far apply equally to every kind of community. However, should you be a city dweller, your considerations are going to be slightly different than they are for those people who live in rural areas or the suburbs because you are going to confront different kinds of structures.

Buildings and property

Whether you live in a city, suburban community, or in the countryside, notice the sizes and shapes of the buildings and homes. Look for potential poison arrows whether man-made or natural.

Urban environments

In the city, can you find an apartment in a building that overlooks a park? Do buildings that are higher than your home surround you? If

so, make sure that your main front door does not face the other buildings. You may have to relocate the front door to the side. Is there a
triangular-shaped roof pointing at your front door from the next house
or building? If possible, reposition the door to another location.

When there are two large buildings beside your home or office
building, they can adversely affect the location between them. This is
a poison arrow. In Chapter 5, we discussed common problems and
how you can cure this one. A couple of remedies are available. First,
affix a convex mirror on each side of your building to deflect negative
energy. Then install a tall flagpole or a tall lamppost (if appropriate)
in front of your building. This cure "lifts" chi upwards.

Figure 6.2. An urban poison arrow.

Suburban or rural environments

The shape of your property is an important influence on your energy. In general, square or rectangular shapes work best, with deeper being better than wider. This allows for more potential development and privacy for the homeowner. A lot wider in the front than in the back can make holding onto possessions and money more difficult than a site that is narrower in the front and wider in the back.

Choose a building or location that is elevated relative to the surrounding area, street, and neighborhood; use landscaping, walls, or fences to provide protection to the back and sides of the site. A pie-shaped or L-shaped lot, also known as a flag-lot, are more troublesome. If the shape of your property is challenging, you can make it look more regular by adding outside lights, planting tall trees, and installing flag poles. Ideally the house should be situated on the property so that the front yard and the backyard are in equilibrium.

If you are fortunate enough to be building a new home on a site, you can take advantage of its natural energy, making sure to build in the most auspicious location.

Carrie's story

Carrie lived in a house on the northeast corner of an intersection. Although her home had a nice, clean appearance, it felt as if it sat right on top of the intersection because cars were so frequently driving by. There were no trees, boulders, or fencing to slow the chi from whizzing past the house in both directions. Personally, Carrie felt as though her life was flying by and she was too busy to enjoy any of it. Also, her marriage felt shaky. Her husband Steve suffered from frequent bouts of anger and depression.

She needed to slow down the chi around her home and to attract positive influences. The quickest and easiest remedy was planting several evergreen trees in the corner of her yard nearest the intersection. She also installed attractive fencing and planted shrubs along it, rimming the corner along the intersection. The fencing and trees deflected and absorbed the fast-flowing negative chi from the intersection. Then, after she planted red flowers around the doorway to match those that now rimmed the front yard, positive chi began to find its way to the front door. Each improvement slowly grounded Carrie in the present, allowing her to slow down and just "be." As Steve helped her plant, he began to feel more centered and stable. Thus their relationship and well-being improved.

Streets and roads

As you saw in Carrie's case, the flow of traffic along streets and roadways can be a potent factor in the energy of a location. Here are some common examples to watch out for:

Poison arrows

Straight roads create poison arrows if they aim towards your location. As we have already discussed, direct lines and sharp angles are the source of sharp, cutting chi. These poison arrows could result in misfortune, illness, and bad luck. The degree of the negative chi increases when the road runs downhill towards your house, particularly if it is directed towards your front door. It can zoom right into the house.

You can alleviate negative cutting chi by planting bushes or trees along the roadway. But remember not to plant them directly in front of your entrance or obstructing the door. You can also build a curving wall and plant vines or bushes in front of it.

Busy intersections

If your home is built at an intersection of two streets, it can attract negative chi. It is preferable to avoid busy streets. Intersections tend to be more active than isolated thoroughfares.

A home or building situated opposite a T- or Y-intersection can receive intense blasts of energy that may result in unwanted and unfortunate accidents. (See Figure 6.3A.) Simple remedies to block and absorb the negative energy of these feng shui problems include fences, walls, or landscaping.

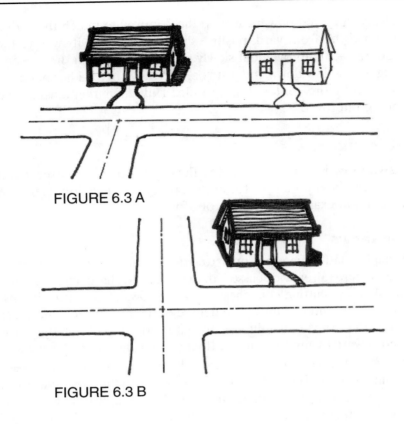

FIGURE 6.3 A

FIGURE 6.3 B

Figure 6.3. Examples of a T-shaped street and busy intersection.

Begin to notice the quality and balance of the chi flowing through the streets and roads where you live. The behavior of people who use those roads and streets is significant. Are your community's streets clean and quiet, or noisy and littered? Notice if your home is surrounded on all sides by roads. If so, plant trees behind the house to give it support. Alleys around and between properties can be a potential source of noise and inappropriate activities.

Cul de sacs, dead-end streets, and hairpin curves

These slow positive chi. From a feng shui perspective, it can be inauspicious if your house is at the end of one. This scenario dissipates and disperses positive chi before it reaches the house. (See Figure 6.4A.)

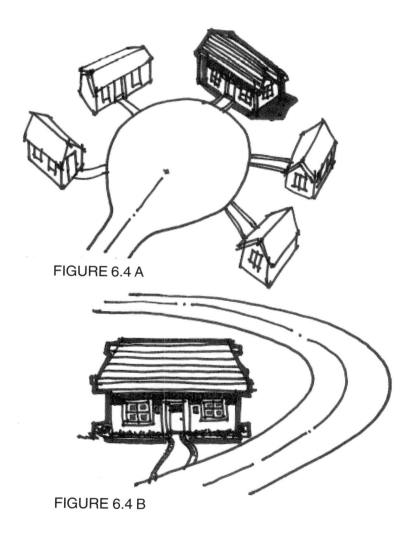

FIGURE 6.4 A

FIGURE 6.4 B

Figure 6.4. Examples of a cul de sac and a hairpin curve.

Toni's Story

Consider Toni's experience. She likes to buy, remodel, and sell houses and has become well known for doing beautiful restorations. In this case, she bought a lovely, old two-story English Tudor home in a sought-after neighborhood. Although the property had suffered from many years of neglect and needed repairs, she felt excited and challenged by the prospect of turning this property into a beauty. But it had a problem she hadn't considered before her purchase. The home was located on the deep inside curve of a sloping road, so that cars going either way, driving up or down the hill, would shine their headlights right inside it at night (see Figure 6.4B). It soon became evident that negative chi was affecting both Toni and her construction crew. She felt tired, irritable, and unorganized. Her contractors weren't showing up as scheduled or on time, and they were going over budget. She needed to mitigate the negative chi quickly.

Fortunately, Toni had planned for a large remodeling and was able to budget in the remedies she needed. She built a tall stucco wall to surround the curve. She then planted tall bushes around the wall, along with grape ivy that clung along the stucco. The look was very much in keeping with an English Tudor style. As the wall deflected the negative energy and blocked the annoying headlights at night, Toni's energy revitalized. Even her subcontractors noticed the shift in energy as soon as she completed it. She was able to quickly finish restoring the entire home and property to its original beauty.

What is the energy of your ideal community?

Play with this exercise to determine if the energy of your neighborhood is right for you or if you are planning to move, buy a home in a new area, or are building a new home and feel unsure about the energy of the site. Allow your creativity and heart's desires to flow freely. Start by getting out a plain sheet of paper and some colored pens.

Take a few moments to relax and be still. Close your eyes and breathe deeply. When you are ready, draw your home in the middle of the paper. Because you will be sketching your ideal neighborhood and community, just make this image a small circle or square. Then close your eyes again and imagine.

What is the ideal setting for your home? What would it feel like? Allow all sorts of images to pass through your mind. How rural or urban is your inner vision? Do you sense cool breezes from the mountains or expansive vistas over farmlands? Does your inner eye project a beachside resort or do you visualize and feel the upbeat energy of a contemporary inner-city neighborhood surrounded by upscale restaurants and shops?

I understand that you may prefer a certain kind of energy, such as a rural area would hold, but your family's needs also have to be taken into consideration. Young schoolchildren might require certain amenities that a more developed area provides, for example. What is suitable for the greater good is an important factor, but try not to limit yourself unnecessarily.

Start to draw your ideal community scene around your home on the paper. Sketch in other buildings and homes, hills and waterways, and streets and roads. Include how far or how near you would prefer certain amenities, such as a park, market, church, recreation, fitness club, or café, to be from your location. Sketch in how close you would like your workplace to be. Would you be able to walk to it or would you need to drive or otherwise commute?

Review the five elements. Go back to the list on page 110 depicting what sort of businesses and topography is associated with each one. How do they fit into your ideal scenario? Which elements do you need to add to your picture to keep your surroundings in balance? Consider yin and yang qualities and characteristics.

Sensing the feng shui of a neighborhood or village is more subtle and organic than simply noting the region's physical landscape. A community is also composed of people. So take the time to imagine yourself going into the grocery store, coffee shop, and Laundromat. What are the people there like? How do they make you feel? Friendly, safe, and comfortable? Uneasy, anxious, and irritated? You intuitively know what kind of energy resonates with you and makes you thrive. Now draw your inhabitants in, using symbols to depict their qualities.

Once you have completed your drawing to your own satisfaction—and remember, this exercise should be free-flow without judgment—you may be surprised at how specific the sketch has become. Your sketch is going to help you in your search for a new home and neighborhood because you are going to be more tuned to the subtle energy infusing the different communities you consider. Once you have found an overall area that has good feng shui, it makes it easier to choose the exact location of your apartment, house, or building site.

If you question the importance of doing an exercise like this, remember that it is much easier to install remedies to improve the chi of a single home than it is to install feng shui cures in a whole neighborhood!

Chapter 7

Evaluating Your Home and Garden

Acccoring to feng shui, when the energy in your home flows smoothly, so should your life. Your home is the single best place to begin creating harmony and setting personal intentions, because it is the environment that typically represents the most intimate self. At home, you are the one who selects the furnishings and décor, and as you move around the space you are constantly filling it with your personal chi. Your home thus becomes a literal outward expression of your physical, emotional, and spiritual inner world. Similarly, your belongings and the layouts of the rooms are always imprinting their chi upon you. Everything you touch, see, hear, and smell leaves an impression. You and your home have a unique and dynamic relationship. Therefore the easiest way to change your life may simply be to rearrange the place where you live.

Your garden is an extension of your home that embodies the special potential to assist in improving the dynamics of your life. Because it can be filled with growing plants, flowers, trees, and shrubs, it brings the vital energy of Nature and its seasonal cycles into your realm, as well as the light of the sun, moon, and stars. A carefully tended garden can bring the blessing of positive chi to nourish you and support the goals you set.

In this chapter, you are going to learn to apply to your home and garden what you have already discovered about the bagua, the five elements, and the feng shui remedies for common problems. Begin by walking room by room through your home.

First impressions

Think of the notion of love at first sight. Such chemistry is overwhelming and attractive. Likewise, the first impression of your home has the potential to make a huge impact on anyone who enters it. Your home should create as powerful an influence on guests when they arrive as love does. It should make a clear statement about who you are and how you want others to interact with you. When your main entrance has good feng shui, it may also prompt you to feel better when you venture out into the world.

Because a picture is worth a thousand words, or so they say, what are your walkway, front door, and entry hall saying?

Your walkway

Ideally, the approach to your front door should be clearly defined, wide, and curve towards the entrance. The walkway should be easy to find and well-lit. Your aim is to attract and welcome fortune, prosperity, and opportunity to your door. A spacious, curving walkway allows positive chi to freely flow towards the mouth of chi, which in this case is your front door.

Your entrance is one of the most important aspects of good feng shui. Well-tended flowers or shrubs should enhance your pathway and front door. Shrubbery, overgrowth, and trees that hang near or above the entrance could block positive chi from reaching it. So remove all obstacles. Anything that hinders easy access, whether it is a column or a narrow walkway, can result in negative chi manifesting in the part of your life that is governed by the zone that correlates with your front door.

Also avoid walkways that are too steep or otherwise difficult to traverse. You wouldn't want any loose stones rocking underfoot, for example. Any maintenance issues around your main entrance need to be resolved. Especially imperative are household issues relating to water. It is terrible feng shui to have a leaky faucet, hose bib, or sprinkler system by your front door. Remember: Water represents wealth, cash flow, and emotions! Anything that is broken or stuck therefore needs to be repaired immediately.

When I had new latches installed on the front gate to my yard, the handyman who installed them thought that it would be okay if the gate stuck "a little bit," rubbing tightly against its frame. I called him and explained that it wasn't good feng shui when an entrance doesn't open smoothly. It would hinder positive chi from flowing to my door. He immediately came back and fixed it properly, and within a few days, out of the blue—magically—I received a call from a past client to list her home for sale.

Your front door

The front door is considered your main entrance. Make it as beautiful as you can. Its job is to invite the world into your home. Chi enters through the front door, and you should know by now that you want to entice every bit of good chi into your life that you can. Red doors are great for attracting positive chi. Black, the color associated with your Journey and Career zone, is good, too. Choose whichever color works better with your overall color scheme. Doorways and thresholds are historically and religiously symbolic. It is beneficial to mark the front door with a special sign, symbol, banner, or wreath that has a positive, personal meaning for you.

In addition, be sure that each of the five elements—wood, fire, earth, metal, and water—is represented and in balance around the door. Begin the journey of bringing the positive energy of harmony into your home at the front door. Your doorway should have a view of the street or front yard so that you can see who is approaching. The most auspicious entrances are situated at ground level or elevated from the street.

Make sure your door is clean. Do the hinges creak? Does it need to be repainted? An attractive, secure, and aesthetically pleasing front door with locks and hardware in good condition will contribute to a more successful life. Does the doorbell operate? Is there a pleasing chime to it? Is your doormat falling apart? Be sure there is adequate lighting when it is dark. If you hang a living thing on your door, such as a wreath, make sure to replace it when it becomes dead and brittle. The idea is to attract opportunity and fortune through your front door, not death and decay.

Your entry hall

The entry hall is the face of your home. It reveals your story and should create a special atmosphere. Let it also establish the spirit and character of your home. What do you want to express? A spacious foyer can foster a transition when you first walk in the door from the busy pace of your work-a-day world to tranquility and a home in which to refresh, renew, and relax.

Make your entry hall or foyer a focal point. Furniture in the foyer can foster a comfortable atmosphere. If your entry is large enough for a table, keep fresh flowers or a beautiful plant on one. Beckon Mother Nature into your home. The elements of Nature are abundant with positive and life-enhancing energy. The vista just inside an entrance door determines how energy will flow throughout a home.

When your entry is small and has a wall immediately in front of the entrance, consider hanging a framed mirror there. If the first thing you were to see upon entering was that blank wall, it would stop your flow of chi as though you were running into a brick wall. You would feel stuck and unable to move forward easily. If you prefer not to use a mirror in your foyer, you could hang a picture of a landscape or a waterfall instead. An area rug is another good idea to fill this space. Incorporate the colors that correlate to the zone of the bagua that your entry lies within, such as blue tones for Self-Wisdom and Knowledge, black for Journey and Career, or shades of gray for Helpful Friends and Travel.

Interior floor plans

Once inside, what is the first thing you see? Stairways that directly face the door can be associated with difficulty in managing money or maintaining important relationships. In such cases, the chi comes through the front door and immediately disperses up or down the stairs. This is also the effect when your front door is in alignment with a door on the other side of the house or when there is a large window directly in view from the front door. To remedy these kinds of problems, you can hang a wind chime or a crystal inside the doorway to slow down the chi and keep it from running out of the house. To achieve the same result, you can also place a piece of furniture or a screen in your foyer.

As a feng shui Realtor, I am often called upon to give advice to home sellers and their real-estate agents. Once a very successful Realtor in Santa Barbara asked me to come to a new listing and share my expertise with her sellers. They had received a feng shui consultation years earlier when they first moved into the home and installed a cure in their foyer. Because the foyer opened onto a spacious living room with large picture windows at the far end, the owners had placed a lovely Chinese table with a large and beautiful statue set upon it to block the view. In other words, if the table and statue were removed, your first impression would be a lovely and expansive vista of the pool and mountains.

Most real estate agents would have counseled their sellers to remove the table and statue, so that potential buyers would be immediately impressed with the view upon entering the home. As a Realtor for more than 20 years, I understand this idea. On the surface, it sounds perfectly logical. However, this is a situation where positive energy would definitely run straight out the window if there weren't something there to block it from escaping. For confirmation, I asked the owners if there had been a significant change when they had placed the table and statue in the foyer. Indeed, their relationship had become more loving and intimate and their prosperity had shot through the roof.

I counseled the sellers to leave the table and statue where they were. Any potential buyers would certainly feel the positive energy suffusing their home. I believed the harmony and enchantment of their home would be an even larger sales feature than the magnificent view. They left the furniture placed as it was, and, sure enough, the home went into escrow within a couple of weeks.

Here are some floor plans to consider:

- When the first room you can see from the entrance is the living room or dining room, you will more likely feel a comfortable sense of transition from the outside world to the inner harbor of home and hearth.

- When the kitchen is the first room you can see, you may often end up being unconsciously drawn there to eat.

- When the bathroom is what you can see first, you may frequently have the urge to use it. Remember that bathrooms are also associated with water and symbolic of money and emotions. This placement of the bathroom could indicate that your money and emotions are draining away or being stopped up.

- When bedrooms are the first rooms you can see, you may notice that you are spending too much time sleeping and have low energy.

- A home office or den would be a good placement across from the entrance. As a result, you may find yourself and your children putting a little extra effort into your work and studies.

Interior rooms

Your living room

More than any other room in your home, your living room governs the kind of people you attract. How you handle the decoration of your living room can influence many critical aspects of your life, from friendships and family relationships to success and prosperity. The placement of your furniture is of utmost importance. Seating arrangements should create a sense of security, community, and comfort for both your guests and your family. Your main seating area should be placed so that you can see who is entering the room from where you are sitting.

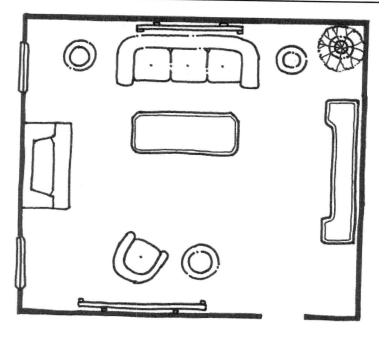

Figure 7.1. An example of good living room placement.

The living room is an ideal place to display your treasures, and it is important to choose your art, antiques, and decorative objects with care. When you place something in your home, you bring that object's energy into your life. So be discriminating. Don't take home *anything* that gives you a negative feeling. To assess the energy of an antique, place your hand very closely over it. Close your eyes and take a long quiet moment to feel the energy of its past. Choose artwork that represents life and happiness. Pieces that depict death or negative experiences should be avoided.

An important focal element in any living room is its fireplace. But the fireplace can allow the chi to escape right up the chimney and out of the house. That would not be good for the inhabitants. Hanging a mirror over the fireplace serves to reflect chi and send it back into the room. Also, when your fireplace is not in use, place a decorative screen or a plant in front of it, and keep wood in the fireplace. These remedies would serve to block the flow of escaping chi.

Your dining room

Do you find it interesting that most formal dining rooms are underused? The reason is that they usually feature two doors or openings and have at least one large window. Because most of the seats do not have solid walls behind them, the environment feels subtly uncomfortable for diners. One cure is to furnish the room with high-backed chairs.

When your dining room is an open area that forms an L-shape with your living room, the space subtly can also feel too open and uncomfortable. You can create more privacy and a heightened sense of comfort in both rooms by placing a floor screen or indoor trees to provide a division between the rooms.

A round dining room table symbolizes the circle of life and heavenly blessings. With an even number of chairs, it will feel most comfortable for you and your guests.

Your kitchen

Feng shui practitioners believe that the kitchen is a symbolic source of wealth and well-being in the home. How food is prepared and where it is prepared are part of the process of sustaining our life force and can be a form of meditation. If we are what we eat, then the setting in which we prepare our food is important, too. When your kitchen is arranged appropriately, your health and family will prosper.

As with the rest of your house, the kitchen should be a place that feeds you emotionally. As the room that is used to store and prepare nourishment, the kitchen is a spiritual center of the home. Make sure that it is clutter-free and has abundant light.

The kitchen has a unique feature. It is the only room where water and fire coexist. Both the refrigerator and sink are water-element appliances and the stove is a fire-element appliance. In the art of feng shui, these two elements are considered incompatible. Water douses fire. Therefore, make sure that neither the sink nor the refrigerator is located next to the stove. Close to one another, but not directly adjacent, is ideal. Because the stove relates to your family's prosperity and well-being, you don't want anything touching it that puts a damper on them.

Another rule of thumb is that the cook must to be able to see anyone who enters the kitchen. If your stove faces a wall and the kitchen doorway cannot be seen from the cook's primary work area, place a mirror on the wall in back of the stove to reflect the entrance. This not only restores security to the cook, but it also makes the kitchen feel bigger and symbolically doubles the number of burners, a feng shui tip for magnifying prosperity. Also, make sure that the stove and oven are in good working condition, as they are symbolic of wealth in the home.

Your bedroom

Your bedroom is the most intimate room in your home, a place where you spend much of your time. It is your personal sanctuary. Because the bedroom is your place of retreat, it can symbolize the way you perceive your inner self. Therefore treat your bedroom with love and care. The chi of the bedroom is closely linked to our relationships and physical health.

When your bedroom is dark and dreary, you may have low self-esteem. You could find that decorating with lighter colors, hanging mirrors, and using more lighting tend to uplift your spirits. When your bedroom is too light and bright, you may find yourself giving away your energy to others and never leaving enough for yourself. You could create more of a nest by decorating with warmer colors and toning down the lighting. Is it the last room that you decorated? If so, notice whether you also put yourself last in the world.

You will feel the most safe and secure when your bedroom is placed at the back of the house. Ideally, it should be situated in the area of Marriage and Relationship in the far right-hand corner of the bagua. This zone is most auspicious for enhancing and creating love and romance, marriage and partnerships. It heightens relationships because it holds the receptive, feminine, yin qualities of Mother Earth. Choose cures and enhancements that symbolize and embody the qualities of love.

Bedroom tips to enhance romance

- Choose bedside tables that are approximately the same size, if not matching. This can promote balance and equality in your marriage or relationships. Likewise, allow for ample space on both sides of the bed for access and making the bed.
- Furniture should be rounded. Angular furniture with sharp corners sends out "cutting chi" that can be damaging to your relationship and your health.
- Decorate with one of the following colors: pink, rose, yellow, peach, apricot, terra cotta, lavender, or cream. Use dark colors sparingly and avoid too much gray, white, and silver, because they tend to scatter personal energy.
- Display romantic and/or pleasant and relaxing photographs and artwork. Do not display images of your children here. Their gaze can subtly distract you from being a couple. Choose pictures, photographs, and art that depict loving and happy couples.
- Do not store anything under the bed and be sure that the bed skirts allow for good circulation underneath the bed.
- Create a mood of romance, intimacy, and relaxation with comfortable furnishings, clean bed linens, curtains for privacy, warm area rugs or carpeting, and soft lighting.
- Avoid having a TV in the bedroom, unless you can place it in a cabinet or armoire behind a closed door. Also avoid electric blankets, as their energy fields can interfere with your own.
- Only display recent photographs in your bedroom.

You have already removed all unnecessary clutter and unloved objects from your entire home, right? The bedroom door should be able to open fully, so don't hang things on the back of the door, or allow piles of things behind it. This will help you receive the positive chi you want for your relationships. In addition, avoid using your bedroom for other types of activities, such as office work or fitness. The bedroom should be reserved for intimacy, nurturing, security, and sleeping.

An ideal bedroom is square or rectangular so it has no missing zones in the bagua. Although it is best to avoid bedrooms with slanted walls or ceilings, it is more important to avoid bedrooms that have beams on the ceiling. Beams are a common design element, but they can wreak havoc on your health, relationships, and general well-being. Ceiling beams create invisible "cutting chi" that results in numerous problems. For instance, a beam running lengthwise down the bed creates an invisible divide between couples.

Beams can also adversely affect your health. Whichever area of the body they cross over can become weaker. Likewise, ceiling fans located above the bed create "cutting chi." Blades are symbolic of knives. Resulting health problems could be severe. The same advice applies to cupboards, bookshelves, and any kind of built-ins that create a recess at the head of the bed. These send "cutting chi" towards the sleeper, exerting pressure on the head and throat area. Remove anything above your head.

Mirrors in the bedroom should be oval or round. They should also be free of distortion or fading. When you can see yourself in any mirrors while you are lying in bed, you could experience difficulty sleeping, frequent bad dreams, or poor health. If you have sliding closet doors with mirrors attached to them, try installing a curtain that you can close to cover the mirrors at night.

Bed placement

Feng shui places great importance on the position of your bed. Your bed should be located where you can see anyone entering the bedroom. However, it should not be placed directly across from the doorway. The ideal spot would be on a diagonal across from the door. This gives you a good view and a sense of control over your destiny. When your bed is poorly placed, especially opposite the door, nervousness and ill health could follow.

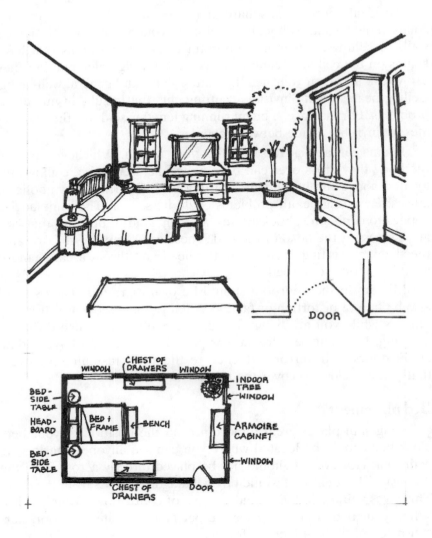

Figure 7.2. An example of good bedroom placement.

Your bed should be securely mounted on a frame with a headboard, as this will provide a secure foundation to your relationships. Then the headboard should be situated against a solid wall to promote a sense of security. Try to avoid having the head of your bed against or underneath a window. Your personal chi could seep out.

Avoid positioning the bed so that your feet are directly pointing towards the door. The Chinese call this the coffin position because the dead are usually removed feet first. It would clearly be an inauspicious way for you to sleep. When you have no alternative, be sure that your bed has a footboard and/or put a bench or trunk at the foot of the bed to slow the chi down.

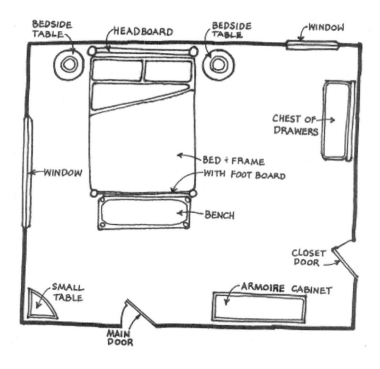

Figure 7.3. Bed in direct line to the door.

Never purchase a mattress with a split down the middle. Don't combine twin beds to make a king-size bed. This type of arrangement sends subtle messages that can deteriorate an intimate relationship. And, while we are discussing mattresses, never keep a mattress after a divorce or when a long-term relationship has ended. The energy field of the former partner is infused in the mattress. Get a new one!

I also highly recommend that you buy a new bed frame for yourself. Antique beds and reused beds contain the energies, both positive and negative, of their previous owners. You must be very careful that you aren't sleeping in a bed that has trauma associated with it. You would be entangling your chi with someone else's negative energy.

Your children's bedrooms

The same essential principles of bed positioning apply to a child's room as well as your bedroom. Also place nothing over the head; avoid beams and overhead fans directly above the bed; and aim mirrors so they do not reflect the sleeper. Help your kids keep their rooms clutter-free by using lots of bins for organizing and storing. Allow them to have a voice in the decorating scheme of their rooms, as they will thrive in an environment that supports their personal energy and resonance.

Children's bedrooms should be painted in soft shades of color. You don't want these to be too cool, as your children could become withdrawn. You also don't want them to be too hot, as your children could become overstimulated. Cool colors are light blues and soft greens. Hot colors are reds, oranges, and bright yellows. Think of cool colors as calming and warm colors as energizing.

As the mother of a child once diagnosed with Attention Deficit Hyperactivity Disorder (ADHD), I spent many years learning everything I could about the syndrome. Children prone to ADHD and Attention Deficit Disorder (ADD) should have bedrooms and playrooms that are pastel. When I look at the bedroom decor for children being advertised in various catalogs, I think it's no wonder so many children feel overstimulated these days.

Your bathroom

Water is a symbol of purity and healing. In many cultures and religious faiths, water represents the immortality of the soul. The principles of feng shui state that the bathroom is one of the most important rooms in the house because it is governed by water. And water, as you have already seen, is closely related to money and the emotions.

When leaks and drips occur, they should be fixed immediately. This is an indication of your prosperity seeping away. Of course, a leaking tap may only mean that you need new washers; however, there is often a correlation between the plumbing and someone's emotional state. If your drains are clogged, it could be a sign that your emotions are blocked. If a toilet overflows, it could be a sign that your emotions are overflowing. Keep drains, toilets, and faucets in good repair. Furthermore, the simple act of cleaning your bathroom and organizing its cabinets can foster renewal and purification in your life.

Bathrooms are best located on an exterior wall of your house. Avoid putting them in the corner bagua zones of either Prosperity and Abundance or Marriage and Relationship, too. When designing a bathroom, be certain that the toilet is out of direct view upon entering your home or the bathroom. Regardless of where the bathroom is located, it is always good to keep the toilet lid closed and the bathroom door closed. Prosperity could flow out of the house through the toilet pipes and the bathroom drains.

Your home office

Our work is a way of expressing spirit. Many of us have home offices these days, places for work and study. In Chapter 8, we will discuss the feng shui principles that pertain to offices of all kinds. An office should be a setting that honors and expresses the qualities of consciousness you offer the world through your vocation.

If you were running a business from your home, the best placement for your home office would either be in the zone of Prosperity and Abundance or of Fame and Reputation. These two areas govern fame, fortune, and prosperity. This would ensure good reputation and success. If the room were a study for your school-aged children, the best results could come from a room in the zone of Self-Wisdom and Knowledge. That zone enhances personal growth and scholarly success.

Gardens

You can magnify happiness and prosperity by applying feng shui principles in your garden. Outdoor feng shui incorporates knowledge of the seasons, climatic conditions, and geography to attract and balance the life force. Remember that feng shui at its simplest means "wind" and "water." So, of course it has much to teach us about our tended landscapes.

Every garden has a unique energy. Many gardens are greatly admired for their flowering beauty and impressive vistas. A cottage garden with informal plantings and intimate spaces might echo the relationship between the soul of the gardener and her garden. Wild natural settings, rather than overly manicured landscapes, increase our innate yearnings to be close to Mother Nature. Eastern cultures have always seen gardens as spiritual landscapes. A garden is a metaphor of the timeless world beyond and expresses the ancient ideal of the mystic-philosopher deep in meditation.

Classical Chinese gardens and traditional feng shui gardens often tend to accent simplicity. A specific area of the garden may focus on one type of plant, or grouping of trees, shrubs, or flowers during a particular season. Feng shui assigns particular influences to the placement, energy, and color of specific plants and flowers, as well as to the five elements in garden design. No matter whether it is a simple and austere Zen garden or a wild natural landscape, your garden is a place to allow your spirit to dwell in the sacred repose of Nature.

Initial steps

Your garden must be clean, inviting, and well-kept. Begin by making sure it is clutter-free. Remove any dead or dying plants immediately. You don't want any "dead" energy. You will find that your garden is influenced by seasonal changes. Warm, dry summer months create different influences than the cold, wet winter months. Therefore, take care to encourage beneficial chi to flourish throughout different seasons. Depending on the nature of your climatic conditions, evergreens, water elements, and lighting can heighten and maintain positive energy during the most challenging months of the year.

Next, be certain to repair or throw away anything in your garden that is broken. This could include furniture, lighting, lawn equipment, and leaky hoses. Also, tend your walkways and steps. Oil squeaky gate hinges; mend and paint your fences.

The bagua in your garden

Next, overlay the bagua on your garden. As usual, orient it to the "mouth of chi," which in this case is the main entrance to your garden. This could be the back door of your house or a gate opening

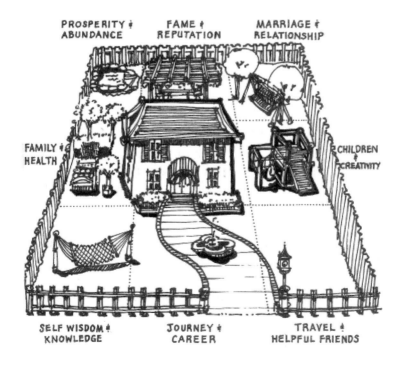

Figure 7.4. Using the bagua for garden placement.

from the sidewalk. But whether it is one of these or a pathway from the street, lay the bagua map so that the most frequently used entrance falls in the zone of (from left to right) Self-Wisdom and Knowledge, Journey and Career, or Helpful Friends and Travel.

Here are a few ways you can empower your life by enhancing the various zones of your garden bagua:

* *Helpful Friends and Travel*: A garden lush with clusters of cornflowers in this zone is said to enhance relationships with friends, clients, and spiritual guides.

* *Journey and Career*: Water symbolizes money, creativity, and inspiration. Install a fountain, waterfall, or fishpond in this zone to benefit your career.

* *Self-Wisdom and Knowledge*: A group of blue lilies of the Nile mixed with yellow day lilies in this zone would promote clear thinking, intelligence, and tranquility. Meditation under a birch tree could also attune you to woodland spirits.

* *Health and Family*: The evergreen yew is associated with protection and the birch tree (known as "the lady of the woods") is a plant totem known for the quality of cleansing. Plant these trees in this area to promote health and well-being.

* *Prosperity and Abundance*: Ferns in this zone are considered auspicious, because they are believed to bring financial success and opportunity. This lacy plant is associated with fairies, luck, and wealth.

* *Fame and Reputation*: Try a rock or stone garden here, where its magical qualities can enhance your personal power and status as well as the landscape. Group pots of red geraniums to further enhance this zone.

* *Marriage and Relationships*: Roses are the flower totems of the heart, governing romance, passion, beauty, divination, and psychic powers. Their thorns teach us that these fragile elements of the heart are not to be grabbed at carelessly. Plant your rose garden in this zone, and put special emphasis on the many shades and types of pink roses that can enhance romance.

* *Children and Creativity*: Daisies are the totem of children, butterflies, and fairies. Cultivate clusters of daisies in this area of your garden to help you feel young at heart and to attract Elves and

Fairies. These elemental spirits are also said to be attracted to anything that reflects light, such as a pond or fountain, or is colorful and moving, such as whirligigs and banners.

U-shaped, L-shaped, or T-shaped dwellings are missing certain zones of the bagua. Outside garden elements can help complete a zone of the bagua that is missing or indented in your home's indoor floor plan. Use lampposts, tall trees, large boulders, upright water fountains and birdbaths, arbors and trellises with climbing vines, or tall garden sculptures to help anchor, extend, and otherwise remedy the problem by symbolically extending and reestablishing the missing area.

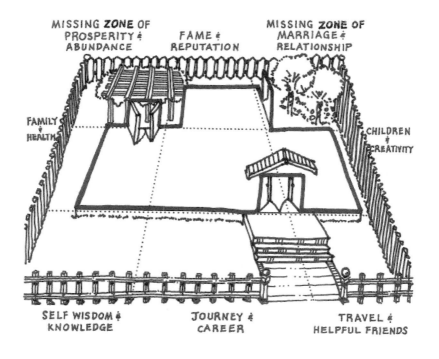

Figure 7.5. Garden cure for a missing bagua zone in the house.

The story of
Adam and Jordan

Adam and Jordan had a gorgeous home in an exclusive neighborhood. They had slowly, lovingly, and meticulously restored the entire house to their personal tastes. Soon it was going to be time to redo the old and tired landscape design. However, the remodeling of the interior of the home had taken its toll on their relationship and on their finances. Even though they were delighted with the results, the process had taken longer and cost more than they had originally intended. Money was tight and they were constantly bickering with each other.

Before landscaping, the couple wanted to put their last dollars into the interior of their home. One of their friends told them about feng shui, so they gave me a call to come over and see what kind of "fine tuning" I could suggest for their house. As we walked around and talked, I soon learned that they were openly concerned about their finances and discreetly concerned about their relationship.

Everything made immediate sense when I saw that the layout of their home was missing the two zones of the bagua that represented their prosperity and their relationship. I gently explained the situation and they agreed with my assessment. Instead of spending their remaining budget on the interior, I recommended that they begin the process of landscaping to cure the missing zones. In this way, they would boost both their romance and their financial prosperity—a good plan.

Next, we set about deciding how each missing zone would best be enhanced. Both Adam and Jordan were talented in creating attractive homes and had a good eye for balance and placement. One idea we came up with together was an atrium for the area representing the zone of Prosperity and Abundance. Coincidentally this meant that they could place French doors in what was then their den/home office, making an especially nice seating area under the atrium for themselves and visitors. We were literally establishing an outdoor "room" in the zone of Prosperity and Abundance.

Next, we looked at the missing area of Marriage and Relationship. On the ground floor, kitchen windows looked out onto this area of the garden from the zone of Creativity and Children. The master bedroom framed the other side of the missing zone, as it was located in the zone of Fame and Reputation. They liked the French doors in their den so much that they also decided to install French doors leading from the bedroom out to the garden. Again, this would create the illusion of an outdoor "room." Still, it needed something more. We decided to place two pink flowering cherry trees in the zone amidst a rose garden. Adam and Jordan chose roses in the colors associated with Marriage and Relationship: pinks, whites, and reds.

By taking these steps, the couple was psychologically able to incorporate and complete the two missing areas of the floor plan of their home. Needless to say, they were enjoined by these two new projects to create love, harmony, and more prosperity in their life together. And, what they sowed, they reaped.

The 5 elements in your garden

You should seek in your garden to balance the representation of the five elements—wood, fire, earth, metal, and water—to harmonize the yin and yang principles. Open, bright yang areas of the garden foster activity. Yin areas of shelter and shade invite quiet sanctuary and solitude. In Chapter 3, we outlined and discussed the various attributes of the five elements. Your goal is to balance them so that no one dominates the others and to use them to stimulate the appropriate movement of chi.

◆ *Wood:* Wood is the force of growth and expansion, just as a tree grows upward towards the sky and the sun, and downward through its roots, which spread out to create strength and stability. Wood is a primary element of the garden, represented by the vertical, columnar shapes of trees. This element embodies the plants and flowers of your garden and it is represented by the color green. In the Cycle of Creation, wood feeds fire. Then, in the Cycle of Destruction, wood consumes the earth, just as trees and plants draw their nutrients from the soil as they grow. You can balance wood with plants and flowers in colors that represent the other elements.

◆ *Metal:* In the Cycle of Creation, metal helps water take form through condensation. In the Cycle of Destruction, metal cuts through wood. Like an axe, metal has the strength to hack through obstacles. Design elements made of metal can bring this element into prominence in your garden. These include metal garden sculptures, including those that spray water, arching gazebos and arbors, and round birdbaths, as well as metal patio furniture, gazing balls, and decorative iron accessories. Use the colors of white, sliver, and gold in cushions or in the petals of resplendent flowers and leaves of plants to further enhance the metal element.

◆ *Earth:* Remember that earth creates metal and dams up water. This element has a powerful stabilizing force. You can find it in square and rectangular shapes, such as those found in decks, railroad ties used as borders around vegetable gardens, or boxed hedges. The earth element is also embodied in terracotta planters, stones and boulders, decorative ceramics, and bricks or tiles used for walkways and patios. Use earth-tone colors such as yellow, cream, peach, orange, and rust to further enhance this element.

◆ *Fire:* In the Cycle of Destruction, fire burns wood, and in the Cycle of Creation, its ashes become earth. Because fire ascends, shapes such as triangles, pyramids, and cones represent it. Fire can light up a dark/yin area where chi may otherwise be too stagnant. Use the color red to increase the fire element or strands of small white lights in the branches of a tree. If you have a missing bagua area outside or inside your home or on your property, an outdoor lamppost can anchor energy there.

◆ *Water:* Water extinguishes fire and feeds wood. This element is symbolic of wealth and money. Black is the color associated with it. Water enhancements include swimming pools, fishponds, cascading fountains, birdbaths, and aquariums. When you have flowing water in your garden, it should flow towards your home to prevent your financial resources from literally and symbolically draining away.

Chapter 8

Evaluating Your Business

Most of us spend longer hours working these days, which means more time spent in the surroundings of our offices. The stress of keeping up with the workload has increased commensurably, so that many people are experiencing work-related illnesses. For these reasons, it is more important than ever for your office building and individual office to be in a state of harmony, conducive to your productivity and health. The good news is that you can use your knowledge of the bagua and the five elements to enhance and remedy the energy of your office building, personal office, and even your desktop. This paves the way for joyous collaboration, abundance, and the career of your dreams.

An initial feng shui assessment

Do you enjoy going to your office each day? Or do you notice your energy shift down a notch or two (with an audible sigh) whenever you enter your workspace? Just as the flow of positive energy in your personal life can be affected and influenced by your home, so too can the qualities of your office influence your chi.

By now, I'm sure you can sense the energy of different places. So consider: What does your office feel like? What do the offices of your coworkers feel like? When your office is comfortable, uplifting, and energizing, these qualities will be reflected in your overall well-being and in your level of production, creativity, and success. Everything you see, sense, feel, or hear, including the colors of the walls and furnishings, the plants, the artwork, and the style and condition of the furnishings and equipment, makes an impact.

Answer the following questions to assess the feng shui of both your company's overall space and your individual office:

+ At the entrance, notice your feelings. Do you feel stronger, uplifted, excited, lighter, and more focused? Or do you feel depressed, pressured, distracted, overwhelmed, and weary? What is your own body language telling you?

+ What is the primary message communicated to you and to others by the company's common areas and by your personal office?

+ When a client comes to your place of business, what judgments do you think he or she makes about your building and your individual office?

+ How do you feel throughout the day when you are working in your office, both in the shared areas and your personal space?

+ What does the energy or spirit of your office seem to be?

Should you find the answers you gave unfavorable, ask a few more questions. You need to be clear about the image you want to project in order to create an environment that supports your vision for your work life.

+ What is the message that you would prefer your office and office building to convey?

+ What essential qualities and energy would you like your office to communicate to your inner being, to your associates, and to your clients?

Now be intentional. Clarify your sense of purpose and what you desire to accomplish in your workspace. Be honest. Be specific. What kind of contribution do you want to make? Are you seeking greater recognition and a promotion? Do you want to increase your income? Would your job go more smoothly if there were greater harmony among the coworkers? Once you have declared your intentions, you can introduce the cures and enhancements that would support them.

Your office building

Those of us who work in office buildings that are smaller than the buildings that surround them need to be especially aware of sharp angles and straight lines. Poison arrows and their cutting chi create negative influences. A good remedy is to place a convex mirror on the outside of your building, where it can "bounce back" to its source any negative chi that is attacking your structure.

An office building located at the end of a dead-end street or a T-shaped intersection is considered a less auspicious location for harmony and prosperity. A good remedy is to plant trees in the ground or in pots around the entrance to the building. This promotes good fortune and expansion. Another remedy is to install a fountain near the entrance to attract wealth and productivity to your company.

The entrance to your building should be in keeping with the overall design and size of the structure. The front door should be well-lit and appear welcoming. For best results, the main door to your company should be located in the middle of the facade, which is in the area of Journey and Career. The energy of this zone of the bagua is preferable for business.

Make sure the reception area is a comfortable, welcoming place for your clients and other visitors. The reception desk should be placed diagonally, rather than directly facing the door. Ideally, this desk should be curved. Otherwise the cutting chi from the corners of the desk could subtly and negatively influence incoming prospects, staff, and guests.

Office pollution and sick-building syndrome are significant problems that will be covered in Chapter 9.

Your personal office

The best location for a private office would be diagonally opposite the main entrance to your company's space, either in the zone of Prosperity and Abundance or in the zone of Marriage and Relationship on the entire floor plan. When you can avoid it, do not locate your office at the end of a long corridor. However, if that is your situation and you do not have the option to move, place a large green plant in the hallway or hang a crystal outside your door. These two remedies can deflect harmful fast chi from racing straight into your office through the corridor.

Other situations to avoid include an office near the entrance, facing a staircase or an escalator, or next to the bathroom. These are energy drainers. When choosing a space within your company's offices, also avoid one next to large office equipment, such as photocopiers. It is advisable to keep your distance from energy-draining electromagnetic fields (EMFs). Ask your office manager to replace fluorescent or halogen lighting with full-spectrum lighting.

Offices should be square or rectangular in shape. If possible, avoid unusual shapes, beams, and obstructing pillars. Of course, you cannot always dictate your choices at work, unless you are the boss! Use mirrors to replace missing and indented zones of the bagua. Make sure that beams are painted the same color as the ceiling above them. Place plants in front of columns or affix mirrors on round pillars to mitigate any negative chi. When office dividers are being used, remedy any sharp edges with mirrors and plants.

Clearing the energy in your office

When you are moving into a new office, the first priority is to conduct an energy-clearing. Clearing the energy in a longtime office is also beneficial on occasion. We discussed several techniques for space-clearing in Chapter 5; nonetheless, I am going to repeat some of those instructions here.

Begin by doing a thorough office cleaning before you attempt space-clearing rituals. Go through your old files and discard any unneeded papers. Box up and store anything that you may need in the future, being sure to get every item of miscellaneous paperwork that is no longer necessary out of the office. Clean out your desk drawers.

As you did when you were uncluttering your home, get rid of anything you don't need or love. Fix anything that is broken.

Next, simplify your space. Organize absolutely everything in your office and everything you need to get done. Arrange places in your desk to keep pens, pencils, paper clips, and any small supplies. This is very important: Create a special folder for items of business that need to be completed, whether they are memos and articles to write, designs to lay out, spreadsheets to calculate, or other projects to complete. Once you have cleaned and organized your office, you are ready to perform a space-clearing ritual.

Space-clearing rituals can often be a little tricky in a place of business. Some coworkers may think you've lost your marbles. Although it is a good idea to respect others sensitivities, I encourage you not to pay too much mind to what people think. It may be better to do a ritual over the weekend or after hours one evening when your coworkers have gone home. Anyway, once they witness the results in your productivity and in your life, they may begin to sit up and take notice. If nothing else, hopefully they will respect your individuality.

Go back to Chapter 5 and repeat one or all of the rituals there for clearing energy. If you do not want to smudge in the office because of the aroma, use a ritual incorporating bells. When you are doing your ritual at a quiet time, other than during regular office hours, and no one will be offended, light a stick of incense. Try sandalwood or (my favorite) nag champa.

To clear the energy of your home, I asked you to recite an affirmation intended to bring in loving and healing energy. In this case, it is preferable to affirm a different intention that would be more appropriate to business. It is always stronger to make up your own affirmations; however, I have prepared a few statements to demonstrate:

- "Golden opportunities and prosperity are drawn to me."
- "I can be as successful as I want to be."
- "I bless this space to abundantly support my creative and financial intentions."
- "My boss and my coworkers are my trusted allies."

Now that the energy of your office has been cleared, you need only to maintain it. During office hours, you can periodically spray the air with an atomizer filled with a light rose or orange scent to uplift and refresh your space.

The 5 elements in your office

Balancing the five elements is an essential aspect of improving the feng shui in your office. You want to make sure there is some of each and that none outshine the others. In addition, each of the elements governs certain kinds of activities and work projects. Once you have identified your job's ruling element, you can enhance it to reach your maximum potential. Let us consider these associations one by one.

Wood

Creative ideas are the seeds of new beginnings and growth. Therefore, strategizing and implementing a marketing campaign to promote the sales of products and information is a job associated with the wood element. Jobs that pertain to the wood element require working in stages from planning a project to following through on it.

Too much wood in your office could result in a sense of being overwhelmed or having too much on your plate and could create an inability to complete projects. Too little wood could result in frustration and the inability to get projects going. To enhance the wood element, use wood furnishings and plants.

Fire

Careers that require high energy and put you in the limelight embody the fire element. Those who work in the entertainment industry, sports figures, advertising and public relations, and some types of salespeople therefore would benefit from enhancing their office chi with the attributes of fire, which governs enthusiasm and activity.

Overuse of the fire element could lead to "burn out" and the feeling that you are losing ground to your competitors. Underuse could prevent you from keeping up. To activate the fire element, choose art that depicts wildlife, use red accessories, or add a lighting element, such as a table or floor lamp.

Earth

Professions in the service industries, such as real estate and healthcare, are aligned with the element of earth. Earth governs hospital workers, doctors, nurses, and social workers. It also rules jobs in industries that directly correlate to the resources of the earth—land, trees, gardens, minerals, gems, and ores, such as home building, landscaping, mining, and the delivery of energy. Placing attributes of the earth element in the workplace can amplify the productivity and success of these individuals.

An overabundance of earth would be typical of someone "stuck in the mud" and in the past, a "pack rat" holding onto his or her stuff, who is not able to simplify. A deficit of earth could indicate a lack of stability and grounding. Energize the earth element with pottery, creamy colors, or a quartz crystal.

Metal

Jobs that require management skills, product development, and corporate follow-through are represented by the metal element. Introducing more of the metal element into the working environment can foster careers such as bookkeeping and scientific research, which necessitate detail and analysis. Likewise, work related to travel, such as jobs in airlines, shipping, and recreation, is also enhanced by metal.

Too much metal could cause distractions and an inability to concentrate and focus. Too little could result in sloppy thinking and a lack of specificity. Magnify the metal element with a metal lamp base or a metal filing cabinet.

Water

The water element is characteristic of visionary thinkers, writers, artists, healers, and academics. People whose work requires invention, intuition, innovation, and creativity would find their contributions encouraged by emphasizing attributes of the water element in their workplaces.

Too much water energy could result in depression and an inability to maintain focus and attention, literally feeling "watered-down" or "washed up." Too little and your ideas could "dry up." Your imagination wouldn't flow freely. To enhance the water element, install a small fountain or aquarium.

The location of your desk

Where you situate your furniture has a profound influence on the energy of your office and what you want to create there. Good placement makes an impact on your relationships with clients and coworkers, fostering good will, a solid reputation, and prosperity. Simply moving your desk can often result in a major shift in your ability to focus and be productive, and therefore your success in your industry.

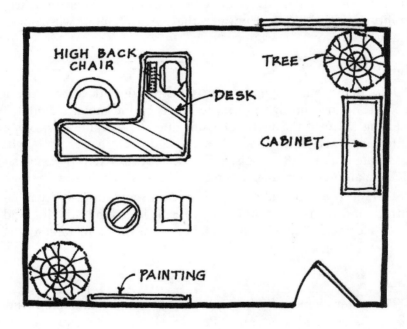

Figure 8.1. An example of good placement in the office.

The most important consideration is the position of your workspace or desk in relationship to the door. Position your desk towards the back of the room where you can see the door without being directly in the path of chi entering the room. From this catercorner spot, you can easily identify visitors and view the entire room. This position is known as the "position of power," because it fosters feelings of control and security.

When it is not possible to place your desk in the position of power, remedy the situation by strategically placing a mirror so that you can see the reflection of the door behind you. Even a small mirror placed on your desk may be beneficial from a psychological point of view. Sitting at a desk that doesn't provide this view of the door could create a sense of things happening behind your back. For the same reason, a high-backed, solid desk chair is recommended.

When possible, also position your desk so that your back is to a solid wall and near enough to a window to allow in natural light. It is even better if your window looks out on an attractive landscape. Avoid sitting with your back to any window. Also be careful if you directly face a window, as your attention can easily be distracted by what's outside. In my real-estate company, because our desks are located beside an interior window, my officemate and I have installed attractive wooden blinds. This remedy allows light in and gives our private office a sense of openness, while keeping the passersby from distracting us. We found that the energy in the room shifted the moment the blinds were installed.

Cubicles have become commonplace features of modern office design. If you work in an "open plan" environment, your increased awareness of the energy and feng shui of your work area is the most important enhancement of all. Because you want to avoid a desk that directly faces a wall, attach a small convex mirror to the upper corner of your computer monitor. This remedy will give you enough wide-angle reflection to restore your sense of security. Otherwise you would likely feel blocked and face frequent obstacles.

In addition, avoid having metal file cabinets and bookshelves behind you. Their poison arrows can weaken your position in your company. If you can, use bookshelves that are not exposed. Put cabinet doors on them. Shelves behind and above your head that are filled with books, manuals, or files can lead to feelings of oppression, pressure, and stress. Should they be unavoidable, place draping vine-like plants on the shelves and the corners of the cabinets.

In a conference room, a round table is much more conducive to cooperation and creativity than an angular one. It sends the message, "We are working together." Rectangular conference tables, on the other hand, project the message of being a detail-oriented and no-nonsense operation and getting work done expeditiously. When you are the one running a meeting, sit in a position at the table where you can see the door. Remember, this is the position of power.

 ## Barb's story

Barb worked in the corporate headquarters of a large financial institution where she was senior vice president of the marketing department. She called me to help her improve the feng shui of her office. Business was booming, yet there was never enough time for her to get caught up. She was overwhelmed. Projects were mounting and she felt unable to delegate as much as she would have liked. In addition, her personal life was suffering because she was either at work or she was thinking about work. It had been about 10 years since her divorce and she wanted to have a relationship again.

During our first consultation I found that Barb had a large and spacious office, but it was so crammed with papers, documents, files, and piles that I couldn't see how she could make heads or tails of her work. Just uncluttering the office was going to be our biggest task to begin. Fortunately, she was able to ask a secretary on her staff to help her tackle the organization of her files and paperwork. Two immense metal filing cabinets were situated on either side of the doorway. We had them removed and set up in a storeroom near her office. Then it took three weeks to get her office cleaned out and uncluttered, but it was worth it!

When I returned for our second consultation, which I call "phase two," Barb greeted me with a big smile. Already she was feeling much better. By removing the mountains of papers and files and seemingly incomplete projects from her office, Barb was finally able to get them resolved one by one. She had been giving more tasks to her assistant, who put the list of her outstanding projects on Barb's computer. It was easier for Barb to manage, complete, and also to delegate projects now that she didn't have them all silently screaming for her attention every time she walked into the room. Overwhelm—out the door! Barb felt more in control and emotionally centered than she had in years.

Next we got to work on the placement of her furnishings. Because her desk faced the open door directly, negative chi was blowing straight at her. We moved the desk so that it was on a diagonal line with the mouth of chi. Because Barb was already financially successful, we intentionally chose to put her desk in the zone of Marriage and Relationship. As a further enhancement, we placed two beautifully upholstered chairs in front of her desk with a small end table between them. This made a comfortable seating arrangement for meetings with her clients and staff.

In the corner of Prosperity and Abundance we placed a large, healthy, green indoor tree. In the zone of Helpful Friends and Travel we decided to hang several pieces of attractive framed art depicting luxurious and relaxing travel destinations. We moved a bookcase into the zone of Self-Wisdom and Knowledge and arranged books, small plants, pictures, and other objects there to support Barb's interest in education and self-improvement. For several hours we circled around her office, arranging and rearranging her belongings, creatively playing together to activate and foster the life she wanted to build. After a while, we sat down to relax and drink a cup of tea. We looked around the room and realized that a slow transformation was taking place. Barb's face shone with both anticipation and exhaustion. I could literally see her personal energy shifting.

Then we spent some extra time enhancing her zone of Marriage and Relationship in the baguas of both her office and desktop. Barb purchased a classy rose-colored vase to hold fresh pink flowers and situated it on her desk. She also found a magnificent piece of raw rose quartz to use as a paperweight. Barb had been so pleased with the results after we uncluttered and reorganized her office that she was determined to ground her new intention for romance as strongly as possible.

Well, you can guess what happened! Within the next two weeks her company merged with another successful company and the new CEO was making the rounds to meet with all the senior management. When this gentleman came into her office, he was immediately smitten with Barb (or was it the ambient chi of her office, too?). The rest, they say, is history. They are living happily—so far—ever after.

The bagua in your office

Feng shui offers you an opportunity to shift your way of being within your workplace to manifest a better future. However, modern insights and common sense must combine with ancient wisdom in practical application. For example, it would often be considered inappropriate to accessorize your office with Chinese objects such as hanging crystals, wind chimes, Buddha figurines, fountains, mirrors, and incense. Therefore, in my consultations, I usually emphasize moving existing objects to locations that are more symbolically astute. It is seldom necessary to purchase anything new.

The bagua is going to help you figure out how to improve your office to match your intentions. Begin by drawing a plan of the current layout of your personal office. This should be easier than drawing your home because most offices are boxy. Assuming the shape is square or rectangular, lay the tracing of the bagua map over your office (see Figure 8.2). Notice where your door is located. Does chi enter the room in the zone of Helpful Friends and Travel, Journey and Career, or Self-Wisdom and Knowledge? Look to see where each zone of the bagua is located in relation to the mouth of chi.

Let us assume that you have been able to situate your desk in the position of power, and you can work from there. Next work on the larger pieces of furniture, such as file cabinets, bureaus, or chairs. Can these be moved to enhance their positions? Then move them. Keep your intentions in mind. For instance, it would be ideal for you to place your desk in the zone of Prosperity and Abundance if you wanted to enhance your cash flow. There you would be sitting in the zone that generates wealth and power.

The zone of Fame and Reputation would be a good place to display any awards or symbols of your standing within your industry. To enhance your career reputation or gain a promotion, consider objects or cures that symbolically reflect the self that you want to become.

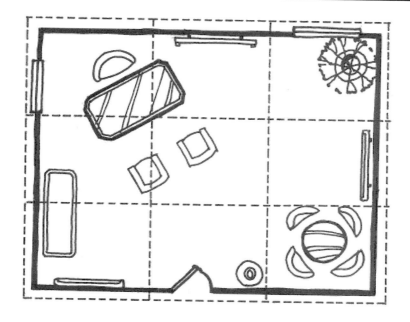

Figure 8.2. Using the bagua for office placement.

Move clockwise to the zone of Marriage and Relationship. Place any photos of your spouse or love partner in this area. Generally speaking, when you want to enhance the romantic aspect of your life, you should predominantly attend to this zone in your home. However, it would be perfectly fine to place discreet, symbolic, and subtle enhancements in your workspace. Remember though, it is your office and it is important to focus most of your attention on your work when you are here.

The next zone to address is Children and Creativity. What you can place here depends on where this falls in your office, specifically whether you are going to place objects of creativity on your desk, a tabletop, or artwork on the walls. If this zone holds your desktop, I would recommend photos of your children. If this zone includes your overall office, then consider artwork that stimulates your creativity.

In order to increase your referrals or be able to take more vacations, place enhancements in the next zone of Helpful Friends and Travel. If your office were big enough to accommodate them, this would be a good spot to have a couple of chairs for visiting clients. Another way to reinforce your intention is to hang pictures on the walls of wonderful travel destinations. When the entrance to your office is in this particular zone, you should attract positive chi coming through the door in the form of clients and referrals.

Does the door to your office open into the zone of Journey and Career? Then an enhancement that boosts your career would be apropos. Do you recall that black is the color associated with this zone and that water is its ruling element? Could you place a small fountain on a table next to the door? Could you paint your door black? Hang a powerful quote on the back of the door, one that has meaning and depth in relation to the path of your career.

There is another possible bagua zone in which your door may be located: Self-Wisdom and Knowledge. If this is the case, consider placing books, periodicals, and magazines on a small table next to the door to reflect your business interests and pursuits. Hang a picture on the wall. Majestic mountains would be a good choice as this zone is ruled by the trigram "Still Mountain."

The last bagua zone in our example is Family and Health. Placing a healthy green plant in this area enhances both family solidarity and physical well-being. If your company were a family-owned business, this would be a good place to honor family tradition, perhaps with photos of your ancestors (especially those who started the business) and your current family. This category could include both your blood relatives and your family of coworkers.

Improving the feng shui of your office can have far-reaching consequences, some of which would be impossible to anticipate. Consider Paul's story.

Paul's story

Paul was the chief financial officer of a large and successful real-estate development firm. He had held this position for a couple of years and really turned around the bottom line. In fact, as a result of his efficiency, reputation, and his warm demeanor, he was often asked by his coworkers to take their issues to the boss. Paul relished his job; however, he knew that his coworkers were being overworked and underappreciated. The staff was just too small to handle the firm's workload. He wanted to do something about it, such as hiring more staff and buying more efficient office equipment, yet he could never get the owner to spend the time, money, and effort needed to address the problem. Although Paul knew he was respected and valued by the owner, he was frequently at odds with him for bringing the matter up. On the advice of some mutual clients, he brought me in for a consultation because he hoped to use the tools of feng shui to communicate better with his boss.

When I came to his office, I noticed that it was located in the company bagua's zone of Helpful Friends and Travel. Furthermore, the door of his office was also located in this same zone of his office bagua. Only in Paul's case, the people coming through the door were seeking his assistance instead of offering support. No wonder he was everyone's "helpful friend," angel, and champion.

Although Paul had a number of other feng shui concerns, we agreed that the most pressing issue in terms of his career was his relationship with the owner of the firm. According to feng shui, the zone of Family and Health corresponds to your elders or those in authority, such as a boss. Thus we laid the bagua map over his floor plan to analyze where this zone was located in his office. Then we evaluated the area.

We discovered that Paul's desk was situated so that his back was to the zone of "elders." In the space itself, there were bookshelves holding an assortment of books, files, business notebooks, and photographs of his friends, children, and personal travels and experiences. In essence, the chi of the elders was being ignored and downplayed.

We started out by simplifying his entire environment. Because the interior design of his office was such that we couldn't move the position of his workspace or shelves, we had to work within the pre-existing layout. We removed objects that weren't conducive to his work life and his "family" at the development company.

Then we concentrated on enhancing the Family and Health zone of the bagua. Paul understood that he wasn't going to be able to change his boss's viewpoint by being aggressive and telling him that he wasn't doing something "right." He needed his boss to see himself as the beneficent elder figure to his staff-family. And it wouldn't hurt if he saw Paul as his friend and ally in that role. Therefore, I suggested that Paul have himself photographed (discreetly) in a pleasant setting with his boss, perhaps at a gathering when his boss was happy and in a positive frame of mind. In addition, to get some group photos of the work force or work "family" in a similarly happy situation, such as a company picnic or holiday gathering. He would nicely frame these photos and arrange them together in the zone of Family and Health. On the shelf next to the photos he would place leafy green plants.

We also wanted to honor his personal wisdom in dealing with the situation at work. Paul told me he admired black-and-white photographic portraits of the great Native American chiefs. We placed a couple of these in the area of Self-Wisdom and Knowledge to enhance and support his own role as an "elder" among the staff.

Finally, we laid the bagua template on the surface of his desk, locating the zone of Family and Health. His desk was narrow with a glass top. There wasn't much space on it to place a large feng shui cure. So, to amplify the chi of Family and Health, we slipped a quote from Abraham Lincoln beneath the glass on the middle left-hand side. It was beautifully handwritten on a green slip of paper. "Let us have faith that right makes might, and in that faith let us to the end dare to do our duty as we understand it." Paul chose the quote because it resonated with him and the situation he wanted to resolve.

I waited a couple of weeks before calling Paul to see how things were going. He confessed that he had only recently been able to have some photos taken and arranged. Yet his boss had noticed the photos right away and seemed pleased to be acknowledged in Paul's workspace. Some weeks after that, Paul told me that his boss was more frequently stopping by his office unannounced just to chat or say hello for a few minutes. Little by little, over the following weeks, the tension seemed to diminish even further. Paul found that whenever he would ask for something on behalf of the office group, the owner was more willing to consider his proposals and eventually tried some of them out.

The ice had finally cracked, so to speak, and the coldness of the office environment was melting away. As the boss began acknowledging and appreciating his workforce by supporting them with new equipment and increased manpower, the entire office thrived. Performance, productivity, earnings, and office harmony were boosted as a result.

Who would have believed that simply rearranging and enhancing one man's office could have made such an impact on the well-being of an entire company?

Your desktop

You can apply the principles of the bagua to your desktop, just as Paul did, in order to anchor and bring forth your intentions. Desks are generally rectangular, so this works very well. Lay the bagua over the top of your desk, aligning the "mouth of chi" with your seating position (see Figure 8.3). You should be pretty familiar with this process by now. It is most likely that you will be sitting in the zone of Journey and Career because most people's chairs are placed in the center of their desks. However some people do sit on the right-hand side or left-hand side, respectively putting them in the zones of Helpful Friends and Travel or Self-Wisdom and Knowledge.

Once you have aligned the bagua, look at your desk. You need to keep in mind what your intentions are for your workspace. What do you have placed in each zone already? Is it in balance? Is it cluttered or dirty? Remember, you must always begin with a clean space. Therefore, remove as much stuff as possible from your desktop. To keep it clutter-free, think small, symbolic, and work-specific. Then proceed from where you sit.

The zone directly in front of you is Journey and Career. It is where you work on what is current, so it's especially important to keep this area clutter-free. As Paul's does, my desk space has a glass top. I am able to slide significant quotes and affirmations under the

Figure 8.3. Desktop placement.

glass directly in front of me. I can easily and frequently refer to them for guidance, focus, and direction.

To your left is the area of Self-Wisdom and Knowledge. What could you place there that would support you in this area of your life? Something that relates to your work and doesn't take up too much space. Your appointment book? Industry journals?

The zone of Family and Health probably won't find much space on your rectangular desk. And let's pray you are not suffering from any significant health challenges. But perhaps there is room for a small, yet healthy green plant.

On the upper left-hand of your desktop, the area of Prosperity and Abundance should be carefully enhanced. What you place here may be determined by your career. Set up a small tabletop water fountain or place a sparkling raw amethyst crystal here.

The upper center of your desk should include an enhancement that fosters your Fame and Reputation, again very important for your career. Try a red cut-glass paperweight. Red activates high energy. Perhaps your business cards in an attractive red card holder?

The zone of Marriage and Relationship is the perfect place to display a photo of your wife, husband, children, or beloved partner. If you would like to bring a loving relationship into your life, put something symbolic of love and romance here, possibly two hearts, two red roses, or a lamp with love birds depicted on it.

In the zone of Creativity and Children, place photos of your children, something one of your children has made, your own artwork, or a work-related object associated with your creativity. On a rectangular-shaped desk, this area may seem a bit small.

The zone of Helpful Friends and Travel is a good spot for your telephone or Rolodex or Palm Pilot. Each of these items embodies your communications with colleagues, clients, and other network of benefactors.

If your desk space needs to accommodate in- and outboxes, your computer, stacks of files, and projects and paperwork that need to be completed and filed, then consider in which zone each of these things would be most auspiciously placed. Should the computer go in Prosperity and Abundance? The stack of files and projects in Self-Wisdom and Knowledge? The in- and outboxes in Marriage and Relationship?

Be sure not to have your desk facing anything or anyone unpleasant. Place a plant or other remedy between you and the unpleasant object. If your desk faces the desk of a fellow associate, place objects of beauty between the two of you to enhance your relationship. Be careful what you put on your desk, avoiding pointed objects. Consider symbols of good fortune, such as flowers or crystal paperweights.

Chapter 9

When You Need an Expert

By now it should be evident that the basic feng shui principles of space-clearing and placement are effective measures for improving the energy of your environment. However, when you are being exposed to harmful chemicals and electromagnetic fields inside your home or on your property, no amount of space-clearing is going to diminish their negative impact. Perhaps you can sense a spiritual presence co-inhabiting your space. Maybe your floor plan is simply too difficult to analyze and remedy on your own, you are buying a home with an uncertain history, or you are suffering a health crisis or going through a challenging period in your life. These are the times when you may need to call upon the specialized knowledge of an expert.

Sick-building syndrome

As a society, we are increasingly aware that chemicals can trigger disease. In fact, illness can be attributed to pollution as often as it is

to infection or genetic factors. A whole new science called environmental medicine has evolved around this issue. Much of the technol-
ogy and materials that were supposed to improve our lives are actually
harming us. Synthetic building materials, electromagnetic fields, and
badly polluted air and water can produce toxic effects inside our work
and dwelling places.

The Environmental Protection Agency estimates that indoor pollution kills more than 11,000 people in the United States every year.
Doctors have linked indoor pollution with ailments that include allergies, joint pain, behavioral problems, kidney disease, and cancer. Right
now, the walls of your home or offices may be emitting formaldehyde,
and your carpets, cabinets, paints, varnishes, and cleaning supplies
may be slowly emitting myriad toxic chemical compounds. No matter
where you live, your indoor air pollution can be 10 times worse than
being outside in Los Angeles on a bad, smog-filled day.

To make matters worse, today's energy-efficient buildings seal in
these toxic gases, which then accumulate and are inhaled or absorbed
through the skin. Therefore, you could be suffering from what is known
as sick-building syndrome. There are a lot of steps you can take on
your own to reduce your toxic exposure. Still there are many sce-
narios where you need help. Let us consider green living first, and
then address the difficult problems.

Green living

Whole books have been written on green living products and self-
sustaining environments. Suffice it to say, it is important to educate
yourself about the amount of harmful chemicals that might be present
in and around your home, including those found in your building and
construction materials, your furnishings, and your household products. Many of these chemicals belong to a group known as volatile
organic compounds (VOCs). Over time, these compounds break down
and leak toxic vapors, both by evaporation and by off gassing. Common VOCs include:

> ◆ *Formaldehyde*: Found in many building materials, at one
> time it was widely used for the insulation of homes. It is
> also used in the manufacture of hundreds of household prod-
> ucts, ranging from fabrics, carpets, and paper products to

cosmetics. This suspected carcinogen causes irritation to the eyes, skin rashes, nosebleeds, headaches, and is linked to chronic fatigue syndrome.

* *Organochlorines*: Found in many household cleaning products and most types of pesticides also contain these compounds. They are suspected carcinogens.

* *Phenols*: Found in a variety of cleaning products and furniture polishes, some are used in stain-resistant coatings applied to furniture fabric. They cause swelling in the bronchial passages, making breathing difficult; rashes and itchy eruptions of the skin; and vomiting.

The best protection you have against toxicity is to buy and use only those items that are beneficial to the health and well-being of your family, your community, and the planet. Here are a few, easy ideas:

* Use nontoxic household products. Manufacturers include Orange Glow Products (*www.greatcleaners.com*), Seventh Generation (*www.seventhgen.com*), and Earth Friendly Products (*www.ecos.com*). Read the book *Better Basics* by Annie Berthold-Bond to find simple recipes for homemade cleaning supplies.

* Instead of wall-to-wall carpeting, use area rugs made of natural fibers, such as cotton and wool.

* Avoid pesticides and air fresheners.

* Store paints, glues, and varnishes in airtight containers.

* Fill your home with living plants, such as spider plants, philodendrons, poinsettias, ficus trees, and English ivy.

What else can you do? Well, green living is a philosophy that holds us accountable for our lifestyles. It encourages us to make choices that support a healthier planet as well as a healthier home, such as recycling, conservation, and self-sustaining systems and materials. Sustainability includes using "off-the-grid" renewable energy sources, such as solar, wind, or waterpower, as well as energy efficiency. You can contact your local energy company to find out about energy conservation measures.

When you are planning to build an eco-friendly home or to renovate your current dwelling place to be more energy-efficient and nontoxic, seek out a specialized architect. Among other questions, ask if your architect ascribes to the principles of baubiology, or building biology, a school of architectural thought that originated in Germany about 20 years ago. The aim of this new science is to create a healthy home that blends elements of the external site and interior design with the principles of deep ecology and the physical and spiritual needs of human beings. It holds a holistic view of the relationship between people and their living environments. The goal is to identify and eliminate the hazards within your current home or before construction. Thus buildings are conceived and built free of any harmful or toxic materials.

To research alternative building and locate architectural resources, contact the U.S. Green Building Council by letter: 1015 18th St. NW, Suite 805, Washington, DC 20036; telephone: (202) 828-7422; or visit the Web site: *www.usgbc.org*. You can contact *Environmental Building News* by letter: 122 Birge Street, Suite 30, Brattleboro, VT 05301; telephone: (802) 257-7300; or visit the Web site: *www.buildinggreen.com*. Contact Livingreen by letter: 218 Helena Avenue, Santa Barbara, CA 93101; telephone: (805) 966-1319; or Web site: *www.livingreen@home.com*. Another good resource to learn more about sustainable living environments is *Natural Home* magazine. Visit their Web site: *www.naturalhomemagazine.com*. Read books published by John and Lynn Marie Bower of the Healthy House Institute (see Recommended Reading) and visit the Web site: *www.hhinst.com*.

Asbestos

Asbestos is a material that was formerly used for insulation and fireproofing. As long as it is properly sealed, it generally doesn't cause problems. But when it is released into the air, particles of asbestos dust are tremendously hazardous. Long-term exposure has been linked to cancer. If your home was built using asbestos, have it removed. I know this can be a time-consuming and costly process. However, it is extremely important.

What can you do? You can hire a certified home inspector or heating contractor to inspect your home for asbestos and, if present, remove it. For your own safety, do not attempt to remove asbestos yourself. Always consult an expert.

Lead

Lead is a toxic metal that can accumulate in the body and lead to brain and nerve damage, as well as contribute to headaches, fatigue, allergies, asthma, and cancer. Young children are especially susceptible to lead poisoning because they are smaller and their brains are still in the process of developing. It has been shown to cause permanent learning disabilities in some cases. Lead is sometimes found in old paints that are peeling off the walls and spreading toxic dust throughout your rooms. Many houses possess old lead pipes, from which metal particles leech into and contaminate the water supply.

What can you do? You can have a plumber replace your lead pipes with copper pipes. If this is too costly an enterprise, install a reverse osmosis water filter for your drinking supply and filtering showerheads. If you suspect lead paint, hire a building contractor to remove it safely and then repaint your home.

Electromagnetic fields

Electromagnetic fields (EMFs) can be found both within and outside your home. Some EMFs originate from radio waves, power lines, radar systems, satellite signals, and cellular antennae sites. The radiation of EMFs is also emitted in lower levels by electronic equipment, such as computers, televisions, plug-in clock radios, microwave ovens, and electric blankets. Although there is some controversy about the hazards of these fields, many scientists have come to believe that frequent proximity to EMFs poses serious health risks. EMFs have been linked, for example, to incidences of cancer and birth defects.

What can you do? First, do not purchase a home near an electrical transformer station or high-voltage electrical lines and cables. If you cannot avoid these power conduits, make sure that your bedroom is located as far away from them as possible. Because we spend so much time sleeping, it is best to limit electrical equipment in the bedroom. Remove or unplug potential sources of EMF radiation. Keep them at least six feet away from your bed, and definitely nowhere near your head. If you suspect that your health has been adversely affected, report it to your local public health department.

In addition, replace your fluorescent lights with full-spectrum lighting that duplicates natural sunlight. Fluorescent lights emit higher levels of electromagnetic radiation. Depending on your exposure and sensitivity, symptoms can include headaches, irritability, eyestrain, and hyperactivity.

Evaluate and diminish your health risks

- What kinds of building materials are used in the construction of your home and its fencing? These may contain volatile organic compounds (VOCs) that can give off fumes when they break down over time. These materials include wallboard, particleboard, laminates and varnishes, paint solvents, pipes, electrical fittings, insulation, adhesives, and wood preservatives.

- *In your living room*: Consider your furnishings, decorations, and building materials. What are your floors made of? Are they wooden? Have you been exposed to stains and varnishes, and do you use floor polishes? Do you have carpeting? If so, what kind? Is it synthetic? Does it have stain-resistant chemical finishes on them? Is it glued to the floor?

  Materials in your home, such as upholstery, curtains, and floor coverings, can contain VOCs that leak toxic invisible vapors. Substitute all-natural materials. Also check to be sure that your fireplace and heating system are in good working condition. These require adequate ventilation.

- *In your bedroom*: Remove sources of EMFs and pollutants. Unplug the TV and use a battery-operated alarm clock. Use an extra blanket instead of an electric blanket. Iron, steel, or metal bed frames and box springs can emit EMFs. Wooden bed frames and mattresses made without metal springs are healthier options. Your bedding may be a source of toxins. Choose bedding that is 100-percent natural.

Evaluate and diminish your health risks (cont'd.)

• *In your kitchen*: Use the microwave oven as little as possible to safe-guard against radiation. Install a reverse osmosis water filter for your drinking and cooking water. The Environmental Protection Agency has cataloged more than 700 pollutants in our drinking water, 20 of them known to be cancer-causing. Be sure that your gas appliances vent prop-erly to the outdoors and are in good operating condition. Metal cook-ware can leach trace elements into your food. Use stainless steel, enamel, or glass pots and pans. Whenever possible avoid using plastics. Plastics contain VOCs and thus can contaminate your food and beverages.

• *In the bathroom*: Avoid using aerosol-type products. Be careful of the paints you choose that may be petrochemical-based or have fungicides in them. Also avoid vinyl wallpaper and PVC flooring. Radon gas can multiply in the bathroom as a result of the warm water. Be sure to have plenty of outside ventilation.

• *In your home office*: When not in use, keep computers and printers, faxes, mobile phones, and any other electrical equipment, such as pho-tocopiers, turned off or even unplugged. That should help protect you from their EMFs. If you have any fluorescent lights, replace them with full-spectrum lighting.

Radon gas

Radon is an odorless and colorless radioactive gas that is carcino-genic, or cancer-causing, when you inhale it. It is more prevalent in certain geological areas than others, where it is found in the rocks, groundwater, and soil. It accounts for up to 50 percent of the radia-tion you could be exposed to from natural sources. And it can seep into your home through your tap water, basement, and foundation.

What can you do? You can purchase a radon home test kit at your local hardware store that enables you to check the radon levels in your home, or you can contact a professional geologist, soil engineer, or radon specialist to do it for you. A specialist knows ways to mini-mize your exposure and prevent radon from entering your home.

Outdoor pollution

Take a quick journey around your property. Are there any electrical power lines or transformers near your home? These are also sources of electromagnetic radiation (see page 167). Is your neighborhood adjacent to any kind of chemical or industrial plant? What about a freeway or even a construction site? These may be sources of air and water pollution. When you are relocating take these circumstances under consideration.

There is not much an individual can do about outdoor pollution except to mitigate its effects indoors or to lobby government officials and agencies to regulate it. Especially when you suffer from allergies, you might consider purchasing a good air filter. Consult your doctor to determine if you are chemically toxic or truly allergic.

Pest control

Many pesticides and fungicides emit harmful VOCs. Although we dispense these chemicals to kill small garden and household pests and organisms, they are also hazardous to people. Some slowly pollute the air we breathe. Others seep into the ground and contaminate the ecosystem. Many popular treatments for termites and dry rot in our buildings also contain deadly chemical compounds.

What can you do? Learn about benevolent insects, such as ladybugs and dragonflies, which can naturally control many of your garden pests. There are numerous organic and biologically safe solutions to prevent pests from damaging your garden. Read books on the subject or consult the staff at your local nursery. To find a newer and safer method to treat termites and dry rot, research companies that specialize in treating these problems efficiently without the use of harmful chemicals.

Geopathic stress

The earth generates numerous fields of energy. Some sacred sites are purposefully built on vortices or ley lines of positive healing energy. Harmful earth energy, on the other hand, can produce unhealthy stresses. Underground streams of flowing water, large mineral deposits, or geological faults deep in the earth may generate abnormal energy fields such as these. Their harmful energy radiates to the surface, where it impacts living things—plants, animals, and human beings.

Geopathic stress affects different people in different ways. Babies, cats, and dogs appear to be more sensitive than adult humans. Cats seem drawn towards sleeping on geopathic stress lines, whereas dogs seem to avoid them. The effect of this kind of stress is usually minimal, unless you spend a longer period sitting or sleeping right above a stress point. In that case, it has the potential to become harmful and debilitating.

Typical symptoms of geopathic stress are frequent irritability, depression, being prone to fatigue, minor illnesses, and migraines, and a susceptibility to other stresses. Many people suspect they have a problem when they feel ill or cannot sleep well when they are at home, but notice that they quickly improve when they are away from their home. Children under geopathic stress may behave erratically and could show signs of Attention Deficit Disorder or hyperactivity.

What can you do? Although methods for testing geopathic stress are often unreliable, you can consult a professional dowser when you suspect that your home is being affected. Dowsers specialize in locating underground water, geopathic stress lines, and geomagnetic ley lines, all of which can influence the energy in your home. Contact a professional society of dowsers to find a reputable experienced practitioner. Try the American Society of Dowsers, P.O. Box 24, Danville, VT 05828; telephone: (802) 684-3417; e-mail: ASD@dowsers.org.

You can also try moving your furniture around. Geopathic stress tends to occur in thin, focused lines, so that a person on one side of a bed could be affected and not someone on the other side. Therefore, the remedy could be as simple as moving your bed or couch out of a line of stress. Even a few feet have the potential to shift you away from the energy caused by underground water. Other actions range from installing cork tiles underneath your bed or sofa (wherever the stress is most symptomatic) to using an insulating blanket or special electronic device underneath the bed to neutralize the area. A traditional remedy is to drive a copper pipe into the ground at a location upstream from the underground source.

 # The story of Sylvia and Bruce

Sylvia and Bruce had me over for a feng shui consultation at their new home. They had purchased the property only a few short months earlier and were stumped about why "things" weren't going right for their 16-year-old son, Jeff. Most teenagers encounter challenges when relocating and changing schools, but Jeff was having a particularly tough time adjusting to their new community. Normally he was a bright, easy-going kid. Now he was suffering from migraines, insomnia, and nightmares. They had already taken him to see a doctor, yet hoped there was another measure that would support his health.

We did a complete feng shui evaluation of the house, placing special emphasis on Jeff's room. Because Sylvia and Bruce were so concerned about their son's well-being, they enthusiastically incorporated the enhancements I recommended. A couple of weeks later, they reported that everything seemed to be going great except that something was still definitely amiss with Jeff. At first I was stumped. Then two things tipped me off to the possibility that the problem might relate to geopathic stress.

Jeff told me that Cody, his beloved golden retriever, wouldn't sleep on his bed since moving to the new house. Then he mentioned that the cat, Xanadu, who had snubbed his bedroom in their former home, had now claimed his bed as her personal snoozing domain. I immediately checked with a local geologist and made a quick call to the city building department to find out if there were any known underground waterways, pipes, natural mineral deposits, or geological fault lines in their neighborhood.

We were amazed to learn, indeed, that running in the ground underneath Jeff's bedroom was a large wastewater pipe serving a large portion of the community. Fortunately, when we moved Jeff's bed to the other side of his room he immediately began sleeping better and his headaches stopped. Cody, the retriever, claimed Jeff's bed back for his snoozes from Xanadu, the cat. And, in no time, Jeff was back to being his old self and making new friends at school.

Spirits/ghosts

When my husband and I lived in western Los Angeles and our first son was a new baby, we bought a house that we thought had great potential as a fixer-upper. It was the most rundown and unkempt property in the neighborhood. No one had lived in it for quite a while and it was in major disrepair and neglect. Early on, I could sense a presence in one particular area of the house. I would not call it a negative energy, although I always felt a little spooked by it. It seemed especially evident at night and during periods when my husband went away for a few days, traveling on business.

One day, while I was gardening in the front yard, a passing neighbor stopped for a chat. As we were discussing the remodeling plans, I mentioned that I believed there was a ghost in the house. My neighbor, who had lived in the area for a long time, shared that the previous owners had felt the same thing and thought an elderly man had once died in the house. "Oh great!" I sighed. Her information explained a recent nightmare about an old man standing at the foot of my bed. It was a lucid dream. Although the man did not appear menacing, I awoke with a jolt, a scream caught tightly in my throat. Of course, I couldn't see him in my waking state. Yet I knew his presence was there.

When we had first moved in, we asked the local priest to come over and bless our home with holy water and prayers. But somehow this old man's spirit was still connected to the house. After the conversation with my neighbor, I consulted a spiritualist who gave me a simple and clear ritual to follow. Each time I felt the presence of the ghost, I would gently say, "This is my house now and it is time for you to go. Your family and friends want to take you home. Ask for them."

After only a few times doing the ritual, I noticed that the old man's presence wasn't around anymore. This simple practice worked!

The presence of a spirit or ghost can make itself known in several ways. Often, one area of a home will feel a little cold and damp, or you will feel a slight prickling sensation along the hairs on your skin. It is usually nothing to be concerned about. Most earth-bound spirits just need gentle encouragement and prodding to seek their own realm of the spirit world. They are having trouble letting go. Talk to them out loud, as you would a friend. Continue to remind the ghost gently but firmly that it can go now. Most of the time you can accomplish removing a ghost on your own.

Another "ghost-busting" method is:

- Clean the room or area thoroughly.
- Sprinkle sea salt in a circle around the entire room, leaving a space in the circle open near a window or door to the outside of the house.
- Talk to the ghost while you are sprinkling. Tell the ghost that it is time to go now. Let the ghost know that the window or door is open for it to leave.
- When you are finished, do not disturb the room for an hour or two. Then come back and close the window or door.

If you are unable to remove an unwanted presence or spirit from your home, ask your priest, rabbi, or other spiritual advisor to come to your home and help you.

When to call a feng shui consultant

After exploring the basics in this book, you may wish to learn more about feng shui. And there may be certain times when the help of an expert in the field can make a difference. I suggest you visit the Feng Shui Warehouse Web site *(www.fengshuiwarehouse.com)* to locate a trained professional in your area.

Weird floor plans

Numerous architects in recent years have played with multilevel design schemes. Sometimes homes are built on challenging lots and the floor plan is an odd shape to accommodate the topography of the land. Perhaps your home has projections and indentations throughout most of the rooms in the house. Maybe you also have an ultramodern dwelling with high ceilings, lots of glass and mirrors, and many sets of stairs leading from one living area to the next. In these cases, you may need the help of an expert feng shui consultant.

You are buying a home

The most important questions to ask your Realtor when considering the purchase of a new home fall under the category of the Predecessor's Law: Why are these people selling/moving? If the previous inhabitants of the home you want to buy enjoyed prosperity and a harmonious family life, then it is more likely that you will as well. If the previous owners are selling because of a divorce, bankruptcy, or, heaven forbid, something traumatic, chances are greater according to the principles of feng shui that you and your family might face similar challenges.

The energy that is embedded in the walls and living spaces from all former occupants is a powerful influence on any new owner. Although space-clearing is advisable whenever you take possession of a new dwelling place, most times it is better for you to choose a property that already has beneficial chi, rather than attempt to cure the overall chi of a home with an unhealthy past.

What is your first *feeling* upon entering the home? Notice your body language. Do you feel uplifted, or are your shoulders sagging? If you are unsure about your instincts, call a feng shui consultant to assist you in making this important decision.

Before you buy your home, you can contact a Realtor who has feng shui training through the Web site*: www.soulstyle.com.*

Extreme health problems

As a culture, the Western world is rapidly beginning to embrace the healing modalities from other cultures, Eastern, indigenous, and ancient. If you should suffer from a serious and challenging illness, consider investigating the many available alternatives to Western medicine. One of these is feng shui. Please remember, however, that it is an adjunct, not a substitute, for a physician's care.

Once you are already doing everything you can medically, working with the energy fields in your home can help align you with beneficial chi. Focus particularly on the Family and Health zone of the bagua in all its respective locations throughout your home. If you do not have good results, then it would be a good time to call in a feng shui consultant.

Unfortunately, there are many issues and lessons that go hand in hand with a challenging illness. These experiences can be difficult, yet are often great teachers. A "dark night of the soul" later usually brings clarity, spiritual rebirth, and entry into the light. My prayers are with you.

Going through a challenging time

Boy oh boy, we all have those times, don't we? Life can be pretty tough. If you have placed cures in the life zones of the bagua within which your difficulties reside, and you have done one or more space-clearing rituals, and you are *still* not having any results, then it would be time to call in a feng shui expert.

Remember that it is important to set a clear intention whenever you are placing cures. Say a prayer or hold an affirmation in mind and be thankful for the blessings you are about to receive from the universe. Gratitude can work like magic.

Conclusion

Feng shui has the potential to change your life. As you free up and generate more beneficial chi, you are going to grow in every way. You may even expect one result and discover another path that is more beneficial than what you had first imagined.

After placing remedies to attract balance and beneficial chi, small improvements should begin right away. However, it is common to have one full cycle of the moon pass before all the results start to pour in (approximately a month). Do not remove a cure you have placed if at first things seem to get worse! Trust that this may be exactly what needed to occur to release the energetic blockage that was holding back your bounty.

Remember that with feng shui, as in all your life endeavors, it is not the final destination, but the *journey* that is to be enjoyed and nurtured. This ancient art is a powerful tool for gaining awareness and self-knowledge. So look within yourself for your answers. Please understand that you hold the keys of transformation and destiny. As within, so without. As without, so within.

Recommended Reading

Alexander, Jane. *Spirit of the Home.* New York: Watson-Guptill, 2000.

Berthold-Bond, Annie. *Better Basics for the Home.* New York: Three Rivers Press, 1999.

Bower, John. *Healthy House Building.* Bloomington, Ind.: The Healthy House Institute, 2000.

Bower, John and Bower, Lynn Marie. *The Healthy House Answer Book.* Bloomington, Ind.: The Healthy House Institute, 1997.

Breathnach, Sarah Ban. *Simple Abundance.* New York: Warner Books, 1995.

Bridges, Carol. *A Soul in Place.* Nashville, Tenn.: Earth Nation Publishing, 1995.

Chiazzari, Suzy. *The Complete Book of Color.* Boston, Mass.: Element Books, 1999.

Chopra, Deepak. *The Way of the Wizard.* New York: Harmony Books, 1995.

Collins, Terah Kathryn. *The Western Guide to Feng Shui.* Carlsbad, Calif.: Hay House, 1997.

Cruden, Loren. *The Spirit of Place.* Vermont: Destiny Books, 1995.

Dadd, Debra Lynn. *Home Safe Home.* New York: Putnam, 1997.

Ferrucci, Piero. *Inevitable Grace.* New York: Putnam, 1990.

Hay, Louise. *You Can Heal Your Life.* Carlsbad, Calif.: Hay House, 1999.

Hillman, James. *The Soul's Code.* New York: Warner, 1996.

Jung, C.G. *Memories, Dreams, Reflections.* New York: Random House, 1961.

Kingston, Karen. *Clear Your Clutter with Feng Shui.* New York: Broadway Books, 1999.

——. *Creating Sacred Space with Feng Shui.* London: Piatkus Books, 1996.

Kron, Joan. *Home-Psych.* New York: Clarkson Potter, 1983.

Lawlor, Anthony. *A Home for the Soul.* New York: Clarkson Potter, 1997.

——. *The Temple in the House.* New York: Putnam, 1994.

Linn, Denise. *Feng Shui for the Soul.* Carlsbad, Calif.: Hay House, 1999.

——. *Sacred Space.* London: Rider, 1995.

——. *Space Clearing.* Chicago, Ill.: Contemporary Books, 2000.

Marcus, Clare Cooper. *House as a Mirror of Self.* Berkeley, Calif.: Conari Press, 1995.

Mitchell, Jann. *Home Sweeter Home.* Hillsboro, Oreg.: Beyond Words Publishing, 1996.

Moore, Thomas. *Care of the Soul.* New York: HarperCollins, 1992.

——. *The Re-Enchantment of Everyday Life.* New York: HarperCollins, 1997.

Moran, Victoria. *Shelter for the Spirit.* New York: HarperCollins, 1997.

Pearson, David. *The Natural House Book.* London: Gaia, 1989.

SantoPietro, Nancy, *Feng Shui: Harmony by Design.* New York: Perigee Books, 1996.

Spear, William. *Feng Shui Made Easy.* London: Thorsons, 1995.

Thornton, James. *A Field Guide to the Soul.* New York: Bell Tower Books, 1999.

Tolle, Eckart. *The Power of Now.* Novato, Calif.: New World Library, 1999.

Tompkins, Peter. The *Secret Life of Nature.* New York: HarperCollins, 1997.

Too, Lillian. *Practical Feng Shui.* Boston, Mass.: Element Books, 2000.

Walsch, Neale Donald. *Conversations With God.* New York: Putnam, 1996.

Webster, Richard. *Feng Shui for Beginners.* New York: Llewellyn, 1989.

Wydra, Nancilee. *Feng Shui in the Garden.* Chicago, Ill.: Contemporary Books, 1997.

Yount, David. *Spiritual Simplicity.* New York: Simon & Schuster, 1997.

Zukav, Gary. *The Seat of the Soul.* New York: Fireside, 1990.

Index

A

A Streetcar Named Desire, 69
airports, 111
American Society of Dowsers, 171
arrows, poison, 84-86, 115
asbestos, 166-167
astrology, Chinese, 24
attention, where you put your, 11

B

bagua in your office, 154-156
bagua zones, 58, 60-70
bagua, 13, 16, 24, 25, 57-73, 159
  how to use, 59-60

bagua, garden, 137-139
  enhancing the zones of your, 138-139
balance, 14-15, 29-39, 41-42, 73
balance, divine, 34
bathroom,
  evaluating your, 135
  problems with the, 89
baubiolgy, 166
bed placement, 131-133
bed, problems with the, 87-88
bedroom tips to enhance romance, 130
bedroom, evaluating your, 129-134
bedrooms, children's, evaluating your, 134
bells as a feng shui cure, 94

bells, 82

belongings, categories for, 78-79

Berthold-Bond, Annie, 165

Better Basics, 165

biology, building, 166

Black Hat Sect, the, 25-26

Book of Changes, the, 24, 57

Bower, John, 166

Bower, Lynn Marie, 166

Buddha, 62

Buddhism, 25

building biology, 166

business, evaluating your, 143-161

C

cedar, 82

cemeteries, 111

Central America, 82

Ch'ien, 69

change, 30-31

Chen, 63

chi, 11-13, 16, 33, 84-92, 92-100,
121-139, 154

chi, mouth of, identifying the,
59-60

chi, the five elements of, 41-46

Children and Creativity zone,
68-69, 92
affirmations for, 101
enhancing, 68, 138-139

Chinese astrology, 24

clapping, 81-82

cleaning, spring, 80

clutter,
clearing your, 76-80
identifying you, 76-77
reducing your, 77-79

color as a feng shui cure, 96

colors, the essence of, 97

community, the energy of your
ideal, 118-120

Compass School the, 24-25

compounds, volatile organic,
164-165, 168, 170

Confucius, 31

Conquest, Cycle of, 51

contemplation, 33, 62

copal, 82

creation, conscious, 11

Creation, Cycle of, 15, 49-51, 52,
53, 142

crystals as a feng shui cure, 99

cul de sacs, 117

cures, feng shui. 92-100

curves, hairpin, 117

Cycle of Conquest, 51

Cycle of Creation, 15, 49-51, 52,
53, 142

Cycle of Destruction, 15, 49, 51,
52, 53, 142

D

dark areas, problems with, 86

desk, the location of your, 150-152

desktop, 159-161

Destruction, Cycle of, 15, 49, 51,
52, 53, 142

dining room, evaluating your, 128
divine balance, 34
door, front, problems with the, 86
doorways problems with, 86-87
Dubois, Blanche, 69

E

Earth Friendly Products, 165
earth, 15, 44, 142, 149
electrical transformers, 112
electromagnetic fields, 167-168
elements, 15, 20, 118
    attributes of the, 49
    balancing the five, 46
    the dominant, reducing in
        your home, 53-54
    the five in your garden, 141
    the five in your office, 148-150
    the, enhancing in your home,
        52-53
    the, evaluating in your home,
        47-49
    the, in your community, 110
energy fields, 12
energy objects as a feng shui
cure, 998
energy, 19
entry hall, evaluating your, 124
environment,
    evaluating the natural, 105-109
    mapping the, 15
    mapping your, 57-73
Environmental Building News, 166
Environmental Protection
    Agency, the, 164, 169

F

Fame and Reputation zone,
    65-66, 91
    enhancing, 66
Family and Health zone, 62-64, 91
    affirmations for, 101
    enhancing, 63, 138-139
fauna, 107-109
feathers, 83
feng schui,
    schools of, 20
    fundamentals of, 14-16
    the definition of, 20
    the origins of, 19
    the universal energy of, 11
feng shui consultant, when to
    call, 174-176
feng shui cures, 92-100
feng shui problems, common,
    84-92
feng shui remedies, installing,
    100-101
Feng Shui, Intuitive, 27
Feng Shui, Landscape, 20-22
fire, 15, 43-44, 142, 148
floor plan, drawing a, 59
floor plans,
    interior, 124-126
    odd-shaped, 70, 174-175
flora, 107-109
Form School, the, 20-22
formaldehyde, 164-165
frankincense, 82

front door,
    evaluating your, 123-124
    problems with the, 86

G

garden bagua, 137-139
    enhancing the zones of your,
    138-139
garden, evaluating your, 136-139
gemstones as a feng shui cure,
    99
geopathic stress, 170-172
    symptoms of, 171
ghosts, 173-174
green living, 164-166

H

hairpin curves, 117
hallways problems with, 86-87
harmony, 29-39
health problems, extreme,
    175-176
health risks, evaluating and
    diminishing your, 168-169
Heaven, Latter, 51
Helpful Friends and Travel
    zone, 69-70, 92
    affirmations for, 101
    enhancing, 70, 138-139
hills, 106
His, Fu, 31, 41, 42
home buying, 175

home office, evaluating your,
    135-136
home,
    enhancing the elements in
    your, 52-53
    evaluating the elements in
    your, 47-49
    evaluating your, 121-136
    reducing the dominant
elements in your, 53-54
hospitals, 111
housekeeping, 80
human spirit, the journey of the,
    38-39

I

I Ching, 24, 57, 58, 60, 61, 63, 64,
    65, 66, 68, 69
indoor pollution, 164
intentions, 16
interior floor plans, 124-126
intersections, busy, 115
intuition, 27
Intuitive Feng Shui, 27

J

Jesus, 62
Journey and Career zone, 60-61,
    90
    affirmations for, 100
    enhancing, 61, 138-139
journey of the human spirit,
    the, 38-39

K

K'an, 60
K'un, 66, 67
Ken, 61
kitchen, evaluating your, 128-129

L

Landscape Feng Shui, 20-22
Latter Heaven, 51
lead, 167
leaks, problems with, 89
Li, 65
Linn, Denise, 83
living room, evaluating your, 126-128
living, green, 164-166
Livingreen, 166

M

mapping the environment, 15
mapping your environment, 57-73
Marriage and Relationship zone, 66-67, 91
    affirmations for, 101
    enhancing, 67, 138-139
meditation, 33, 62
metal, 15, 44-45, 142, 149
Mexico, 82
Mohammed, 62
Mother Teresa, 62
mouth of chi, identifying, 59-60

moving objects as a feng shui cure, 97-98
music as a feng shui cure, 94
myrrh, 82

N

Native Americans, 99
natural environment, evaluating the, 105-109
Natural Home magazine, 166
nature as a feng shui cure, 95
neighborhood, assessing the energy of your, 109-112

O

objects,
    energy as a feng shui cure, 98
    heavy as a feng shui cure, 95-96
    light and bright as a feng shui cure, 92-94
    moving as a feng shui cure, 97-98
office building, evaluating your, 145
office,
    clearing the energy in your, 146-148
    your personal, evaluating, 146-156
office, home, evaluating your, 135-136
opportunity, 11
Orange Glow Products, 165

organochlorines, 165
outdoor pollution, 170

P

pakua, 24
pest control, 170
phenols, 165
placement, bed, 131-133
play, the spirit of, 17
poison arrows, 84-86, 115
police stations, 111
pollution,
    indoor, 164
    outdoor, 170
power stations, 112
prayer, 33, 62
prisons, 111
problems, common feng shui,
    84-92
problems, health, extreme,
    175-176
Prosperity and Abundance
    zone, 64-65, 91
    affirmations for, 101
    enhancing, 64-65, 138-139

R

radon gas, 169
railroad tracks, 111
rituals, space-clearing, 80-84, 147
roads, 115
romance, tips to enhance
    bedroom, 130

S

Sacred Space, 83
sage, 82
salt, 81
Santa Barbara, 106
School, the Compass, 24-25
School, the Form, 20-22
science, modern, 11
Sect, the Black Hat, 25-26
self-inquiry, 62
Self-Wisdom and Knowledge
    zone, 61-62
    affirmations for, 100
    enhancing, 62, 90-91, 138-139
Seventh Generation, 165
Shamans, 19-20
Shamans, Celtic, 99
sick-building syndrome, 163-164
smudge stick, 83
smudging, 82-84
soul selves, 29
sound as a feng shui cure, 94
space-clearinig rituals, 80-84, 147
spirit, the journey of the
    human, 38-39
spirits, 173-174
spring cleaning, 80
stillness, 33
streets, 115
    dead-end, 117
stress, geopathic, 170-172
    symptoms of, 171
structures, assessing, 112-117

Sun, 64
surroundings, evaluating your, 105-120
sweet grass, 82
syndrome, sick-building, 163-164

T

tai chi circle of wholeness, 33
Taoism, 25
totems as a feng shui cure, 99-100
transformers, electrical, 112
Tsu, Lao, 31
Tui, 68

U

U.S. Green Building Center, 166
universe, the oneness of the, 12

V

volatile organic compounds, 164-165, 168, 170

W

walkway, evaluating your, 122-123
water as a feng shui cure, 98-99
water, 15, 45-46, 142, 149-150
waterways, 106-107
wholeness, tai chi circle of, 33
wireless antenna sites, 112
wood, 15, 42-43, 141-142, 148

Y

yang, 14, 33-36
  attributes of, 36
yin, 14, 33-36
  attributes of, 36
Yun, Professor Thomas Lin, 25

Z

zones, missing, 89

About the Author

S hawne Mitchell is a leading feng shui consultant, Realtor, writer, speaker, and workshop leader based in Santa Barbara, California. Over the past 20 years, through her consulting practice, she has helped hundreds of clients find and create life-affirming home and office environments. She may be contacted via her Web site: *www.soulstyle.com.*

Shawne is the former Home Sanctuary Editor for *Healing Retreats and Spas* magazine, for which she contributed regular feature articles and the column "Ask Shawne." Her writing has also appeared in magazines such as *Whole Life Times, Feng Shui Journal, Magical Blend, Casa Classic Homes*, and the *Santa Barbara News Press*, and in the spiritual anthology *More Hot Chocolate for the Mystical Soul.*

A graduate of the University of Washington, Shawne is a candidate for a master's degree in spiritual psychology. She received her feng shui training in the classic tradition of the Black Hat Sect of Tantric Buddhism. She has been a practitioner of Transcendental Meditation for 25 years.